THE
EVOLUTION
OF
WEALTH

*An Economic History of Innovation and Capitalism,
the Role of Government, and the Hazards of Democracy*

JERRY D. WARD

ISBN: 0985012609
ISBN 13: 9780985012601
Library of Congress Control Number: 2012930310
Del Cerro Publishing
San Diego, California

DEDICATION

To my wife, Penny, with love

CONTENTS

Part II
FUTURE EVOLUTION:
Where Do We Go From Here?

INTRODUCTION

We live in the age of abundance.

Well, some of us do. If you were born in the wrong country you are out of luck. Almost four-fifths of the world's population would be grateful to live at the level we define as poverty.

What magic has made us so relatively wealthy, and left so many behind? The most common explanation is that we live in a capitalist nation and they do not. Or some will say it's because the Industrial Revolution happened in England and not in Bangladesh.

Both explanations are true, but unsatisfying. What is it about the capitalist economic system that has made it so successful in creating wealth? If it is so successful, then why is capitalism so disliked and mistrusted by so many people?

More fundamentally, what is capitalism and where did it come from? Why did the Industrial Revolution happen in the Western World and not in China? Why, for the average person, was there almost no improvement in material well-being for thousands and thousands of years, then, in the last three hundred, the rate of change accelerated, bringing some of us wealth beyond the wildest fantasies of any Roman Emperor?

The answers to these questions emerge from the history of our economic system's evolution. This story illuminates how people's natural behavior gave rise to particular economic practices, and hopefully gives better insight into the whole process of change and the production of wealth.

Change is the operative word—the only word that encapsulates this remarkable transition. The instrument of that change, almost by definition, has been successive innovations: the introduction into use of new inventions and new ways of doing things. *The history of economic progress is the history of innovation.*

We are at NOW in this ever-more-rapidly evolving world. Our economy has become the envy of the world. The old socialist and communist nations that did not follow the path of free market capitalism failed completely, both economically and culturally. Now many of these nations, lured by capitalist abundance, have begun to adopt capitalist practices, and it is working. Most have a long way to go, but the odds favor the twenty-first century becoming the Capitalist Century.

It will be a fiercely competitive world. There will be many, many highly motivated young people in the new capitalist countries working long hours for very modest pay to gain their share of this new abundance. It will also be a physically more dangerous world, as envious nations and sects misdirect their emotions and energies.

There is a serious question whether our nation is prepared for this more competitive and dangerous world. Our K-12 educational system falls woefully short. We have too many citizens who have only a vague—and often incorrect—notion of how a capitalistic economy functions. We have large enclaves of mostly minorities not integrated into the fabric of the nation. We seem to have great difficulty in governing ourselves prudently: our politicians spend too much, promise too much, interfere too much, bestow entitlements that we cannot afford, and detract from healthy private sector competition by exceeding their proper role as economic referees and becoming inept players.

Our collective instinct is to blame government. Is prudent budgeting so hard? Are problems like badly performing schools so difficult to fix? Is it reasonable to think that, year after year, the nation has selected the five hundred or so persons to be our federal leaders who are the only citizens unable to face hard, unpleasant problems and do something about them? Could it be that the problem does not lie in the inadequacy of politicians, but in the nature of the system in which they must perform?

Ours is a democracy; the people chose their government. There is wide divergence in our views as to its proper role, and if agreement is to ever be found it is still in the far future. But there is not wide disagreement that at whatever level the government operates it should be honest, prudent, and capable of coping with both problems and opportunities as they arise. Getting that government requires a citizenry motivated to demand such behavior, and sufficiently educated to understand the implications of their vote. That is not impossible to make happen; it is primarily a problem of reshaping incentives. Roughly the last half of the book is focused on such issues in our continuing evolution.

I hope you find the book interesting and thought provoking.

PART I

EVOLUTION PAST

CHAPTER I - THE FIRST TEN THOUSAND YEARS

It wasn't recorded, but the transaction probably went down something like this: Grok traded a stone axe-head for five of Brik's rabbits. That little scene imagined from long ago illustrates almost all of the economic practices that are central to our wealth today.[1]

First, there is specialization, the division of labor. Neither man was trying to be self-sufficient; Grok made axe-heads and Brik was a hunter. By trading, they each got the benefit of the other's expertise; both were better-off exchanging the products of their respective skills than if each tried to do both hunting and axe-head making.

The exchange created satisfaction for both of them. Grok placed more value on five rabbits than he did on his axe-head, and Brik needed an axe-head more than five rabbits, so they both consider themselves better off after the trade. Trade exploits the differing values placed on things by different people.

Trading—buying and selling, now that money has been invented—seems natural to us today. But to the best of my knowledge we are the only species that routinely and freely indulges in such complex quid pro quo trade.[2] It is an innovation from deep

---

1   Of course it was imagined, but it doesn't strain credulity: "Primitive man lived in a state of political autonomy and economic freedom ... . His basic behavior was that of the self-interested individualist." Thomas Mayor, Hunter Gathers: The Original Libertarians. (*The Independent Review*, vol. 16, Num. 4, Spring 2012) 498

2   Some primates have been observed trading grooming for sex or food; apparently they haven't gotten around to inventing money. Kevin Voigt, Monkey Business: Jungle Economics, CNN, November 4, 2009.

in our history, and has a profound and fundamental impact on our economic well being.

Also implicit in that scene is the process that brought our lives out of raw nature. The axe-head that Grok made started as a rock. Some thousands of years earlier it would have stayed a rock. Over time people developed the creativity to make it into an axe-head—an early example of successful technological innovation.[3]

Focus on that word innovation; it is the backbone of this story. It is innovation—the introduction of new things and new ways of doing old things better—that has brought us from caves to the almost unbelievable prosperity the Western world enjoys today.

Technological innovation is the kind of innovation that has put tools in our hands and given us electricity and jet engines and penicillin. *Behavioral innovation* refers to changes in how people work, organize, and interact.

The two work together. Behavioral innovations in the roles of government have permitted the evolution of cultures and climates supportive of technological innovation. Innovations in finance provided access to funds to support the entrepreneur, the innovator. Innovations in business organizations allowed the effective use of new devices that technological innovation has brought forth; for example, it required an entirely new type of organization to run the railroads that the invention of the steam-driven locomotive had made possible.

Successive innovations accumulating over time have multiplied human productivity in every dimension of living, lengthening our lives and providing us with all the comforts and capabilities of modern life. The merit of those practices we call free-market capitalism stems from the fact that these practices have been more supportive of innovation than any other type of economic system the world has ever tried.

---

3   *Invention* is the conception and sometimes the demonstration of something new; it becomes an innovation only when introduced into practice.

The recounting here of the evolution of this development recalls only as much history as is needed to give context to the unfolding story. If you want to know about the Battle of Waterloo or the Treaty of Versailles, this is the wrong book.

Agriculture and Its Implications

Brik and Grok and their contemporaries fed themselves by hunting and foraging. This required a large territory to produce much food, so groups had to stay small, just a single family or at most a small tribe. Total world population was thought to be only a few million people.[4]

Then at the tail end of the last big ice age, some twelve thousand years ago, people in the Middle East and along the Nile started the serious transition from hunting and foraging to agriculture, humankind's first mega-innovation.[5] Our story focuses on this time and region because it is the start of the path that leads to capitalism and the modern world.

The introduction of agriculture resulted in a huge improvement in the *productivity of land* in food production. The amount of land hunter-gatherers needed to feed a small group was enough for farmers to feed much larger settlements. And, as farming spread, so did people begin to reorganize they way they lived.

A time-lapse movie of this reorganization would show many small bands of hunters and foragers coalescing very slowly into small villages. As the *productivity of labor* in farming improved, some farmers could produce an excess over their own needs. This allowed others to abandon farming to do other things, to focus on other dimensions of living. These people tended to agglomerate for mutual support and interaction, and began turning some of

---

4   All population figures are based on data from Vaughn's Summaries, World Population Growth History (Updated 2012)

5   Within a few millennia this transition to agriculture was also starting in the Indus River Valley and along the Yellow River in China, and much later still, in the Americas.

the agricultural villages into small towns and, very slowly, into the world's first cities.

The productivity of agricultural labor may well have been the most important metric for gauging early societies' potential for material progress.

There seems a certain arbitrariness in deciding just when growing population groups became cities. But about five thousand years ago many population centers had begun to fit our idea of a city; they had organized governments, were capable of joint and cooperative action, were home to a variety of skills, and were centers of both production and trading activity. They had begun intensive year-round agriculture in their hinterlands, using coordinated labor forces to build irrigation systems. These were city-states, each with its own independent government. Nations would come later.

Change had been glacial; it took roughly five to six thousand years from the first appearance of early agricultural villages to the establishment of the first cities. Even at the end of this long gestation, it is estimated that nine out of ten people were still farmers.[6]

It is almost impossible to project ourselves into the world and circumstances of that ancient past, when life had to be hard almost beyond our imagination. We have no basis to criticize the rate of advance. A sharpened stick was probably the first farm implement. There were no metals for making tools; stone, wood, animal parts, and clay were the primary raw materials available. There was much to learn, and each small group had to learn and relearn much of it for themselves.

But learn they did. They learned to divert rivers to irrigate fields, to drain swamps, to make and use crude wooden plows, and to use oxen to pull them.[7] They had the ingenuity to turn the stem of the flax plant into linen, the world's first cloth. They learned to use the

---

6   David Christian, *Big History: The Big Bang, Life on Earth, and the Rise of Humanity*, (2008)."As a rule of thumb, in most agrarian civilizations, it took about nine peasants to support one city-dweller." Part 3, p 79.

7   A history of the tools and techniques of agriculture throughout the world is described by Evans, *Feeding the Ten Billion*, (1998).

fleece of domesticated sheep to make a different kind of fabric. They learned to make clay receptacles and kilns hot enough to fire them. These kilns were an important breakthrough; hard clay pots to hold liquids and to keep rats out of the grain were big steps in improving productivity.

The limits of humankind's ability to turn creative thought into reality are primarily restricted by two things. First, what one can make depends very much on the materials available with which to make it. By the time of the first cities man had learned to make bronze, but its primary application was in weaponry, not plows.

The second is the power available to accomplish physical tasks. Very early agricultural man had domesticated the ox, and had learned to use its muscles to supplement his own. They also had horses, but not yet all the gear needed to make them either good draft animals or good transportation.

Five thousand years is still a very long time, and progress may still seem terribly slow, but we have to remember that we are the only species to get even this far on this uncharted evolutionary journey. By the time of the first cities the rate of world population growth had accelerated from almost none to an average increase of something like ten thousand people per year. The many, many separate innovations we now lump together as agriculture was the start.

The City—5000 Years Ago

The city easily qualifies as humankind's second mega-innovation. It was a crucial step toward our modern world, perhaps the most important we have ever known. The city allowed people to learn from each other, to behave collectively on a large scale, and to share a much broader palette of knowledge and experience. The city created choices. The city made possible more extensive mixing of the gene pool. The city significantly changed the trajectory of human development in every dimension of living. The city has been the venue for nearly all of the innovation that has figuratively brought us out of the jungle.

There was a price. Cities were unhealthy places; crowded living with inadequate sanitation was hospitable to disease. And the predominantly cereal-based diet from agriculture was less healthful than the more varied diet provided by foraging; the archaeological evidence showed more bad teeth, decreased stature, and other signs of nutritional deficiencies after agriculture and cities than before.[8] There might well have been additional stresses from living with too much togetherness.

The first cities grew where the earliest transition to agriculture had taken place: in ancient Sumer in Mesopotamia—now Iraq—and in Egypt along the Nile.[9]

Early on the need for commercial record keeping led to the development of the cuneiform type of writing. Cuneiform was a way to depict numbers and objects. Other systems were developed to represent the sounds of talking. Finally, alphabetical language let much fewer symbols be used to construct the sounds.[10]

Before writing, the only way to preserve knowledge was through memory and the only way to transmit it was through face-to-face encounter. The evolving innovation of writing has obviously been a crucial key to mankind's progress.

The Economic Advantages of Growing Markets

The farmer or the forager, in contact with few other people, had to be largely self-sufficient—a jack-of-all-trades. Urban dwellers could specialize much more easily. Archaeologists working in Sumer have found evidence of cooks, brewers, weavers, builders, tanners,

---

8   Amanda Mummert et al, Robusticity during the agricultural transition: Evidence from the bioarchaeological record, *Journal of Economics and Human Biology*, (2011)

9   Jared Diamond, *Guns, Germs, and Steel: The Fates of Human Societies*, (1999) 100

10   The first alphabets are attributed to the Canaanites and the Phoenicians, at this point still fifteen hundred to two thousand years in our future. G. Carboni, *The History of Writing*, (July 2006)

priests, scribes, and all manner of occupations. The Sumerians by 3000 BC had boats with sails, wheeled carts, looms, and rotating platforms for working pottery.[11]

Specialization leads to efficiency; the man who does nothing but make pottery will make more and better pottery per hour of work than the man who makes a pot every three weeks. Thus the average productivity of labor is greatest if everyone works at some specialty, sells his products, and buys his widgets from the widget maker, his pots from the potter, his cloth from the weavers, and so on. All are better off focusing on their area of expertise, and satisfying their other needs by buying from other specialists.

Big projects, like designing and building an irrigation system, require teams of people, organized and directed by some leader. It seems highly doubtful, though, that anyone attempted to direct or coordinate the day-to-day production and the trading of all the goods and services needed to live. It is probable that, for most of history, people in what we now call the private sector naturally found their own economic niche without direction, and traded their stuff whenever and wherever it was opportune. If you specialize, it doesn't take long to figure out that you won't eat well unless other people want your output and are willing to trade for it. It quickly becomes clear that everyone works to satisfy others, and what your output is worth is not determined by you, but what others are willing to trade for it. So it is in everyone's self-interest to satisfy the self-interest of others. No one directs this activity; order and balance emerge when each person follows their own self-interest, which implies catering to the wants and needs of others. Production and trade take place *as if guided by an invisible hand*.[12] This seems to be instinctive.

---

11   Encyclopedia Britannica, *Sumer*, and Harvey S. Firestone, Jr., *Man on the Move: The Story of Transportation*, (1967), 21, 37

12   The metaphor of the 'invisible hand' as the guide to the activity in a free market was introduced by Adam Smith in his *The Wealth of Nations* in 1776, about 3500 years in our future. I borrowed it from there.

The fact that an economy can run itself without external guidance or design is hard to understand. Without some leader or some committee, who decides how many tanners or how many potters the village—or the city—needs? It's easy; somebody, seeing the tanners aren't very busy but the potters are working all the time, decides his self-interest is better served by becoming a potter.

Local markets formed to facilitate trade. It seems reasonable to assume that these were free markets in which prices were established by negotiation, without coercion. These markets were made much more practical by the invention of money, which somewhere along the line had begun to substitute for barter. With money, Grok wouldn't have had to search for someone who both needed an axe-head and just happened to have the rabbits he wanted. He could have just sold the axe-head to the first person that wanted one, then taken the money and bought some rabbits.

So markets and trade permitted people to reap the very significant efficiency, variety, and quality benefits of specialization. As cities grew, more people implied larger markets, and larger markets could support wider specialization and therefore a greater variety of goods and services. For example, in small markets there were few widgets, because no one could specialize in widget making if they needed to sell ten a week to live and the market was only big enough to need five. But if the market size doubled and the demand went from five to ten, someone could become a full-time widget maker and everybody now had the benefit of having widgets available.

Cities were the engine of improving economic conditions. Professor Howard Saalman, in his book Medieval Cities, described the city as a "tool for the production and exchange of goods and services."[13] One seldom thinks of cities as an economic tool, but the characterization is accurate.

So larger cities produce larger markets, and larger markets enable greater specialization and economies of scale, and therefore

---

13   Howard Saalman. *Medieval Cities*, (1968). Saalman noted that cities may be many other things as well.

its occupants gain increasing wealth. Cities grow with the growth in total population and in the proportion of people freed from farming to do other things. Population growth is inhibited by the available food supply, which, in turn, depends primarily on the agricultural productivity of *land* and the amount of arable *land* available.

Having population growth bumping along the ceiling of the ability to feed everybody was a serious gamble; when the vagaries of nature or the actions of marauding armies impeded the output of food, starvation was too frequently the result. It's understandable that gaining the favor of the gods who were perceived to govern such phenomena was such an important part of life.

Among the richer nations today, much-improved transportation has virtually removed this threat of starvation. Modern man still can't make it rain on cue, but now he can draw on the whole world for his food supplies. Even two thousand years ago sailing ships made it possible for Rome to routinely import Egyptian wheat. But for thousands of years the lack of good transportation limited such possibilities, and the real possibility of food shortages was always lurking in these ancient shadows.

The Next Twenty-Seven Hundred Years

It was a long stretch from the first cities in Sumer around 3000 BC to the Greeks and the Romans. Until 324 BC when Alexander broke up the Persian Empire, life in the Middle East reads like just one empire after another. There were first the Sumerian, then the Akkadian, the Babylonian, the Assyrian, and the Persian—and there were many smaller kingdoms from time to time around the edges: Lydians, Hittites, Canaanites, Dorians, Scythians, Phoenicians... . The Egyptian Kingdom lasted for the whole period until absorbed into the Persian Empire. The area covered by the Persian Empire was huge, running from the Indus River to the Mediterranean, and included Turkey and Egypt.

Reading a history of the period leaves the impression that life must have been very turbulent, filled with battles and mayhem, as one group after another conquered and was conquered. That is probably misleading; remember that this period lasted a long, long time, roughly a hundred and twenty-five generations. By modern standards, most of these empires were very long-lived. The geographical area was vast. I conjecture that many, maybe most, of those ancient people lived out their lives quietly, and except for crop failures, locust swarms, and tax collectors, nothing ever seemed to happen.

From our point of view not much new did happen. New and improved versions of bureaucracies came on the scene, starting from the probably very minimal administrations needed in the Sumerian city-states transitioning to the much larger governments required by the Assyrian and Persian Empires.

There are several universals: all governments need money and all people need rules. Governments funded themselves by extracting 'tributes' from the population, mostly farming peasants. There are horror stories about how mercilessly these tribute collectors behaved sometimes when extracting tributes from those poor people.

Tribute extraction, or transfer, in one form or another, has been very common throughout history. When governments perform this activity on a regular basis, we call them taxes. When donations are totally voluntary, we call them gifts. Victorious generals and Roman governors were very good at extraction. Sometimes it's called rent-seeking. All significant economic activity now falls in one of the four classes: *specialization* in production, *trade* and *tribute transfer* in distribution, and *innovation* in change.

Rules, or laws, probably accumulated over time. The most famous of the time were those organized and literally carved in stone by Hammurabi, the sixth king of Babylon, a little under four thousand years ago in 1772 BC. Roughly half of these laws dealt with commercial activity and contracts.[14] They described the terms that

---

14   *Code of Hammurabi*, Wikipedia.

were acceptable in commercial lending, and spelled out in some detail how profit and risk should be shared between the senior partner furnishing the capital and the entrepreneur or merchant driving the endeavor. They described, for example, how losses should be shared if a building collapsed or a merchant ship sank.[15]

If laws like Hammurabi's were deemed appropriate, it's hard not to believe that the economic system was active and generally free market, free enterprise. Even though a large part of Hammurabi's Code was devoted to it, that is infinitesimal compared to today's rules, so that private sector commercial and innovative activity had to have been far less constrained than now. It isn't much of a stretch to call it capitalistic, because there was free market and there was capital, capital not only from the richer merchants and producers, but also from the priests and the members of the government. Perhaps this was capitalism with only a small "c" because it lacked institutions specifically designed to supply anonymous capital as we have today.

No one designed these economies; they evolved, just as did the cities and their governments. As noted, they came about as a consequence of each person doing what came naturally, following his own self-interest. The existence of Hammurabi's laws tells us that it was discovered early on that sometimes people stretched self-interest a bit too far.

These commercially oriented, urban civilizations would appear to have offered a reasonably good climate for innovation.[16] Commerce includes more than just producing and interchanging goods; trade also enables the exchange of ideas and stimulates thought. Commercial activity breeds competition, and competition is a spur to innovation.

---

15   David S Landes, Joel Mokyr, William J Baumol *The Invention of Enterprise: Entrepreneurship from Ancient Mesopotamia to Modern Times*, (2010). Kindle Edition Chap I—Entrepreneurs: From the Near East Takeoff to the Roman Collapse. Section: Financing Enterprise. Kindle Location 1033.

16   Landes (2010), Chap I Section: Some Myths Regarding the Genesis of Enterprise. Kindle Location 803.

The rural countryside was a less promising venue. The rural environment imposed too much separation between people, making communication and cooperation outside the village more difficult. There was much less opportunity to attract capital. As already mentioned, this circumstance is unfortunate, given the importance of agricultural productivity in determining how many people could be freed from farming to do other things.

Most ancient innovations would probably seem unimportant to us today. We remember the ones that got made into movies—like chariots full of fierce warriors. The wheel itself can't be omitted from mention here, given that its importance is often put right up there with sliced bread. Actually, its importance for transportation back then is probably overrated: the wheel's usefulness was limited because of the lack of good roads. In those times roads were built for walking or horses; they couldn't hold up under the cutting of wheels. Sumer had wheeled carts and wagons in 3000 BC, but it took 1500 years for them to show up on mainland Greece; had they been terribly useful one would think they would have diffused more rapidly.[17]

Twenty-five hundred years is a long time, and one might reasonably ask why there were not more inventions and innovations striking enough to attract our attention.

I conjecture that there were three probable reasons. First, there weren't many people available to do the innovating. Estimates have the population of the world growing from about 12 million people when the first cities appeared to maybe 120 million at the time of Pericles, twenty five hundred years ago.[18] Based on the distribution of people over the globe in more recent times, one might guess that no more than a fifth of these were in the Middle East, the region of our focus here. That implies about 3 million at the time of the first cities, growing to perhaps 30 million at the start of the classical period.

---

17   Firestone (1967) 21-22.
18   Vaughn's Summaries again.

Of this 30 million people, something like 80-90 percent were peasant farmers. Given that rural living provided less opportunity for innovation than an urban environment, these peasants' contributions should be partially discounted. But only partially: many did live in the cities, and it's quite possible that the rural dwellers may have been more innovative than we think, but left no record. For example, the wheelbarrow—usually considered a much later innovation—could have been invented and reinvented many dozens of times and, unless they were made of stone or bronze, such devices would not have survived to excite modern archaeologists. Perhaps a picture on a clay tablet would have informed us, but none have been found.

If we arbitrarily discount the peasant population by, say, 50 percent, the pool of potential innovators was about 2 million people at the time of the first cities, increasing to perhaps 16 million people at the start of the classical period. To put these numbers in perspective, there were about 90 million people in Europe two hundred years *before* the Industrial Revolution. Because the roll of the peasant farmer in late medieval Europe was very different than in the earlier agrarian empires, many of these 90 million could be considered part of the pool of potential innovators.

Obviously these numbers are fuzzy; the people at the time seemed to have given little thought to how badly the folks in their distant future were going to need good numbers to write proper books. Worse, my classification of people as in or out of the innovation pool is conjectural and arbitrary. Even the concept of an *innovation pool* is crude; only a very small percentage of people actually have the flexibility of mind, the dedication, and the support to be successful innovators, and that percentage varies with changing conditions. But with something like a fifth as many people available to do the innovating back then as compared with the period in Europe when, as we shall see, technological innovation was just beginning to noticeably accelerate, it's hard to completely dismiss the difference in numbers of people in the innovation pool as a valid reason for slower innovation during these years.

The second reason innovation was slow was that these ancients were starting from scratch. There were no hardware stores on the corner. There were no metals tougher than bronze. Iron had made its appearance well before the end of the era, but it had a bit of evolving to do before it became obviously superior to bronze for weapons. There was almost no technological foundation to build on, and technological innovation is very much a compounding process.

The third reason is that the culture was reconciled to stasis rather than change, a culture that was shaped by the fact that change was so rare. It's doubtful that the idea that things could be made different ever entered most people's thinking.

I think the last two reasons were the most important. The population figures are not overwhelmingly different from those of England during the Industrial Revolution, when innovation was exploding. But in England a very substantial technical base was in place, and there was a very strong cultural bias supporting innovation and change. But it seems illogical to dismiss population size entirely; it's too easy to argue that with a larger population, events in England would have happened faster.

These early civilizations did leave some impressive structures for which the modern tourist industry is extremely grateful. The arch was an important architectural innovation that came from that era. People then also proved that with just muscles and cleverness they could move some mighty big stones.

By the time the Persian Empire was dismantled, roughly two thousand three hundred years ago, new civilizations were already well established in the Mediterranean basin. The centers of power and progress were moving west.

The Classical World

Many of us were taught that the Greeks and the Romans were the real beginning of our civilized world. That's obviously not completely true, although they certainly did leave very large footprints in the sands of time. Greek philosophy and Greek drama are still powerful today, and Greek science dominated the Middle Ages. The Roman innovations in law, language, and government continue to have a strong influence on us. The public structures these civilizations left behind fill us with admiration and awe.

This classical world did not spring fully formed into existence. Certainly it inherited much from the east, but an important part of its legacy started on an island in the Aegean Sea. Homer told us *"There is a land called Crete, in the midst of the wine-dark sea, a fair, rich land, begirt with water, and therein are many men past counting, and ninety cities."*[19]

Crete was the largest of the Greek Islands, and had been occupied by humans for something like a hundred and thirty thousand years.[20] Now known as Minoans, they used bronze beginning about 3400 BC, and by 2700 BC were playing a role in maritime trade in the eastern Mediterranean. They were the first people to build a navy, becoming the first great sea power in the Mediterranean. Their navy was apparently effective—their cities had no walls. The Minoans laid out trade lines that were to last a thousand years.[21]

These Minoans were a very talented, artistic people who had established a thriving bronze-age civilization. They were supplanted by the Mycenaeans, the early occupants of the Greek mainland who had traded with the Minoans, and who, over time, largely adopted their culture and art. These Greek-speaking Mycenaeans participated in and extended the maritime trade network that had been started by the Minoans, spreading early Greek culture throughout the Mediterranean. Sicily and southern Italy were Greek long before they were Latin.

The Minoans were the first westerners to move the boat and the ship to center stage in this evolutionary story. The next seafarers

---

19   Will Durant, *The Life of Greece*, (1939) 5

20   John N. Wilford, *On Crete, New Evidence of Very Ancient Mariners* The New York Times, 15 Feb 2010

21   Casson, Lionel O. The Ancient Mariners: Seafarers and Sea Fighters in the Mediterranean in Ancient Times, 17-22.

were the Phoenicians. They also had culture built on maritime trading and had established trading posts throughout the whole Mediterranean. Carthage was a Phoenician trading post.

Ships in those days, called galleys, were really very long rowboats, pointed at both ends, with multiple rowers seated on each side. The Phoenicians invented a way to almost double their power: they added a second deck with a second layer of rowers. These new galleys were called biremes. By the time of the Greeks, there would be triremes.[22] These boats had sails, but their sails were very inefficient.

Galleys were long and narrow to make them fast, but they were so full of rowers that there was little room for cargo. So for cargo the Phoenicians developed the "round ship" with fewer rowers and more dependence on sail. It was much slower, but much roomier than the "long ship", the galley. These two kinds of vessels, the "long ship" and the "round ship", continue to sit at the top of the genealogical chart for ships. Subsequent generations of ships were to still reflect in hundreds of different variations the basic compromises inherent in these early types.

For all its dangers and difficulties—and they were legion—transport by water was far easier than by land. Rivers and oceans were the primary arteries of commerce from antiquity until the railroads were introduced not quite two hundred years ago.

Copper, tin (to make bronze), iron tools and iron weapons were common in trade—along with almost anything else of value in those ancient times. A reasonably intact example was discovered by a sponge diver in 1982 about six miles off the southern coast of Turkey. The ship, the Uluburun, was estimated to have been sunk around 1310 BC. It carried some ten tons of copper ingots, a ton of tin, a ton of resin, hardwood, ceramic jars of olives, ingots of blue glass, tortoise shells, elephant tusks, hippopotamus teeth, ostrich eggs, and Canaanite and Mycenaean pottery.[23] Judging from

---

22   Casson, Lionel O. *Ships and Seamanship in the Ancient World* (1995) 57-58.

23   Brian M. Fagan, *World Prehistory: A Brief Introduction*, (2008), 232. A complete, detailed list of the cargo is given in *Uluburun Shipwreck* in Wikipedia.

estimated time of sinking, it could have been either Mycenaean or Phoenician.

Classical Greek civilization started around the fifth century BC and was roughly concurrent with the start of the Roman republic. Both Greek and Roman material lives depended on the same economic practices of earlier civilizations: division of labor, trade and markets, innovation, and tribute extraction. Slavery was common.

In technological innovation—the path to growing productivity and wealth—the Greeks led; they were the inventors of the toothed gear and the waterwheel.[24] Anyone who has visited the Acropolis in Athens knows the Greeks were great architects and builders, and they left their structures all over the Mediterranean basin.

The Romans present more of a mixed bag. Their progress appears to have been largely confined to that which was useful in war, in administration, and in producing the magnificent infrastructure that supported their cities. They became real masters at civil and hydraulic engineering; their buildings, roads, and aqueducts were marvels. They focused on making the city a more pleasant place: enclosed sewerage, paved streets, and public bathhouses. Some upper-class homes had running water, bathrooms, and central heating. If not the inventors of cement, the Romans were the first extensive users in the mortar used in masonry structures.

Roman culture was not encouraging toward the tradesman and the laborer. Roman estates were often left under the supervision of a hired overseer (or sometimes a slave), and only casually directed by their wealthy owners. It was not the best culture for agricultural innovation. The attitude of the rich and elite Romans—the Romans who controlled most of the capital—is revealed by Cicero (106 BC-43 BC): *"Public opinion divides the trades and the professions into the liberal and the vulgar. We condemn the odious occupation of the*

---

24   These waterwheels were not devices to produce power from flowing water, but were used as pumps to lift water out of mines. See *Waterwheels*, Wikipedia (original sources are listed therein).

collector of customs and the usurer, and the base and menial work of unskilled laborers, for the very wages the laborer receives are a badge of slavery. Equally contemptible is the business of the retail dealer, for he cannot succeed unless he is dishonest, and dishonesty is the most shameful thing in the world. The work of the mechanic is also degrading, there is nothing noble about a workshop. The least respectable of all trades are those which minister to pleasure."[25]

Private sector entrepreneurs were inhibited by the social values of the time. It could well be that the farmers, tradesmen, and slaves did have ideas, but without support, motivation, and capital, very little innovative thinking seems to have been acted on.[26]

So in the thousand years between Pericles and the dissolution of the Roman Empire, great strides were made in innovative governance, in warfare, in civil engineering, and in the improvement of the built environment. There was apparently only modest improvement in the productivity of labor in farming and in the production of the other needs of living.

The Path Leads To Europe

The western half of the Roman Empire disintegrated in the fifth century AD. It seemed that the baton of economic progress was being passed from the played-out civilizations around the Mediterranean to the vigorous Franks and Germans of the Atlantic seaboard and northern Europe. The people who were now slated to lead the world in technological advancement for the rest of Western history were the ones the Romans had called barbarians: people who still lived in loosely organized tribes or confederations, and were largely educated only by real life.

---

25   David S. Landes, Joel Mokyr, William J., Baumol, *The Invention of Enterprise: Entrepreneurship from Ancient Mesopotamia to Modern Times*, (2010) Chap I—Entrepreneurs: From the Near East Takeoff to the Roman Collapse. Section: Social Status of Merchants and Entrepreneurs. Kindle Location 972.

26   This assessment is largely derived from Joel Mokyr, *The Lever of Riches*. (1990) Chapter 2

Actually, the baton was not being passed: it had been dropped. In many ways it was like starting over. Roman law, Roman protection, Roman money disappeared, and Roman roads deteriorated. The countryside became dangerously lawless. Long-distance trade stopped, markets and cities shrank. Illiteracy became the norm. The so-called dark ages had begun.

People looked to any leader who could offer them some protection. In some cases their choice fell on lords of old Roman estates who maintained loyal and armed followers. Similarly, the Frankish and Germanic chieftains kept retinues of warriors.

Sometime in the early eighth century the stirrup, introduced from the east, precipitated a major reorganization throughout much of Europe. New technologies quite often precipitate reorganizations of society, but it usually takes more than just something that makes it easier to ride a horse.

The stirrup, attached to a high-backed saddle with a rigid frame to spread weight more equally over a horse's back, allowed a man to swing a sword with full force without falling off, or use the weight of the charging horse to overwhelm his opposition with a lance and still stay aboard.

Covered with protective armor, carrying special shields and weapons designed for fighting on horseback, the horse itself with its armor becoming an early version of the battle tank, these new *knights* were virtually invincible. Every leader wanted some of his warriors to be trained and armed as knights.

The problem was that knights needed special armor and weapons, a large horse of the right breed, leisure time to train, and assistants to help. All that was expensive. It was still a barter economy, so these leaders had no money, but they did have land. The typical arrangement was to give the prospective knight enough land with the serfs to work it so that he could support himself, his family, and his retinue. In return, the knight continued to owe allegiance to his lord.

Now the knight had become not only a fighting man but also the lord of his own manor. The knight would typically train his sons to fight on horseback, who would then naturally be the most qualified to replace the aging father as the fighter as well as the lord of the manor. After several generations the job slid into being hereditary, and the knight became part of nobility—the lower end, but nevertheless nobility.[27]

The feudal estate was a world of its own. There was no money; barter is not practical over long distances, so trade was largely restricted to the bounds of the manor. Predictably, the lord of the manor, the almost invincible knight, grew less interested in serving his lord, whose grandfather might have set up the original deal, and became a power unto himself. Without power, the lord who was originally the central authority, lost influence and power devolved to the many knights. The feudal system had been born.

The whole attitude toward work had changed. The Romans had enjoyed the fruits of labor, but disdained the work that had produced it. The Catholic Church did much to change that perspective. In the early Middle Ages some of the monks were of the educated class—almost all of it, in fact. Monks did manual labor, not without a lot of help, but they did work. As Lynn White, a scholar of medieval technology, noted: "The monk was the first intellectual to get dirt under his fingernails."[28] ("Intellectual" seems a bit strong, but you get the idea.) So by its own behavior the church signaled that the farmer and the manual craftsman were no longer despised, and that productive labor was worthy and approved by the Church.

It's a reasonable conjecture that, under feudal arrangements, the relationships between the peasant and his boss—the lord of the manor or his chief of staff—was much closer than when the authority was a distracted Roman senator or a distant government. The arrangement was that the lord provided protection and land to farm in return for the peasants' labor and allegiance. Often he

---

27   Kenneth R Bartlett, *The Development of European Civilization*, (The Great Courses, The Teaching Company, 2011). Lecture 2

28   Lynn White, *Dynamo and Virgin Reconsidered*, (Cambridge, MA MIT Press, 68. Cited in Mokyr, (1990), 204.

directed how that labor was used, and was very likely to know a lot about the nature of the work. He also had a direct interest in doing things better. That would seem to be a much better climate for innovation than had existed in the past.

Most estates used the heavy wheeled plow, which was thought to have been invented by the Slavs.[29] It was particularly good at turning the heavier wet soils of Europe. These plows were originally pulled by a team of oxen, but after the iron horseshoe and the horse collar were introduced, horses took over.[30]

These heavy plows and the animals to pull them were too expensive for more than one per manor. The work, therefore, had to be cooperative—generally a good climate in which to try to find better ways to do things. One might look upon this as a tiny step toward turning agriculture from a cottage industry into a factory industry, which had to wait nearly a thousand years to happen.[31]

Certainly one of the more important innovations was the introduction of the three-field planting cycle, the idea for which was attributed to Charlemagne (742-814) himself. Instead of the old two-field cycle, in which one is planted and the other allowed to lie fallow for a year, the three-field system had one-third planted in the spring, one-third planted in the fall, and one-third fallow. The result was a greater diversity of crops and an increase in productivity of land by roughly 50 percent.[32]

The feudal system evolved during a time when population was falling. By the end of the tenth century agricultural productivity was improving and the population was now increasing. Reliable money (like the Florentine florin and the Venetian ducat) let trade expand beyond the barter-on-the-manor; now the lords of the manor could

---

29   Thomas F. X. Noble, The Foundations of Western Civilization, (The Great Courses, The Teaching Company, 2002) Lecture 34
30   White, (1962),42.
31   Until farming switched from many small plots to fewer large ones, and was run as a business. This started happening in England, and was well advanced by the eighteenth century.
32   White (1962), 69-76. Part of the gain came from a change in the plowing schedules in the three-field system.

indulge their desires to act and live like the nobility they considered themselves, and buy luxuries from the wider world.

With increasing numbers of people and more of them being freed from the need to farm by improving agricultural labor productivity, the feudal manors became overcrowded. People leaving the manors enabled the rapid growth of towns and cities all over Europe. As cities grew, the prospects continued to improve for a rebirth of long-distance trade.

The knights had assumed most of the power, leading to political fragmentation of much of Europe, but the growth of cities favored the return of power to the lords and incipient kings. Greater centralization of power improved the environment for the reestablishment of the basic structure of Roman law.

To repeat an old message: cities enable greater labor specialization, trade, more exchange of ideas, collective efforts, and active markets. Commerce provides the spur of competition to innovative endeavor. Cities have been the birthplace of nearly all nonagricultural innovation. Feudalism declined as cities grew. Improving agricultural productivity is important because farm surpluses allow the growth and support of cities, the venue that has produced most of the world's wealth.

Increasing trade helped launch a new type of citizen: the successful merchant whose wealth and influence could challenge the nobility. With cities came the seeds of a strong private sector and a middle class.

The Crusades started at the end of the eleventh century and went on sporadically for two hundred years. Equipping and moving the accumulated armies, sometimes as many as several hundred thousand men, was a huge problem, and put an entirely new set of demands on the European economy. All kinds of businesses sprang up to support various aspects of this huge movement; Italian cities in particular grew rich supporting the seaborne traffic. Men searched for better ways to manage businesses; double entry bookkeeping was one of the resulting innovations.

Many of the merchants made wealthy by the crusades became bankers. Banks allowed traveling merchants to deposit money in one location then withdraw it in another, without having to risk having it stolen on the journey. Banks could and did loan money to the powerful, and some banks in Florence became very rich lending money to the Pope. Kings always needed money to build things or fight wars, and banks supplied it, sometimes to their regret. These medieval banks were a bit more entrepreneurial than modern banks can prudently be.

The fourteenth century was truly calamitous for the world and for Europe. First, it was in a period called the little ice age, the only time in modern recorded history that the Baltic Sea froze over, which it did in 1303, 1306, and 1307. Early in the century heavy rains in France had so spoiled crops that people starved. Wars here and there did their bit to make life more miserable. Then in 1347 the Bubonic Plague—the Black Death—was introduced into Europe from Asia. No one knows the death rate for certain; estimates put it at a third of the population. Waves of the plague kept returning during the rest to the century, and by 1400 the population of Europe was reduced by half.[33] Descriptions of the time are horrifying; one wonders how it might compare to nuclear war.

Apparently even the blackest clouds have silver linings. Some of the survivors saw their skills more valued, and their real wages rose. Capital became more concentrated when survivors inherited the estates of the dying. Sources of more concentrated capital were timely; two of the major banks of Europe had failed (the English king Edward III had reneged on a massive loan from the Italian banks of the Bardi and Peruzzi families) just before the plague started, and wiped out a lot of people and the source of a lot of capital.[34] This more concentrated capital helped businesses recover from the banks' failure.

---

33 Tuchman (1978), quoted in a University of Wisconsin paper at http://www.uwgb.edu/dutchs/westtech/x14thc.htm.
34 Bartlett (2011), Lecture 5

By the fifteenth century Europe was back on track. Under Portugal's Prince Henry the Navigator, voyages of exploration were finding their way to the Orient. And at the tail end of the fifteenth century a man named Columbus bumped into a new continent across the Atlantic.[35]

Meanwhile in China

So far this history has focused on the evolutionary trail that first led to modern capitalism. But there were over three times as many Asians as Europeans, and they were far from bit players. In fact, the Chinese were well ahead of the Europeans in technical progress up until the fifteenth century.

By that time China was sending huge fleets of very large, technically advanced sailing ships as far as Africa. (This was some sixty to seventy years before Columbus set off in three very small ships to find China.) Then this progress stopped.

It appears that there was an internal court struggle pitting those who backed the benefits of foreign trade against those who preferred the social purity of isolationism.[36] Social purity won; laws were passed forbidding all but small ships to be built and used. Shipyards closed down.

China was one single empire, tightly and autocratically run through a very large bureaucracy. The private sector was distinctly subservient. Prior to this about-face the government both encouraged and participated in furthering technological innovation. Then, with different ideas, the government and the country turned the other way. Revival did not really begin until after the death of Mao Zedong in the twentieth century.

Jared Diamond wrote: *"These consequences of Europe's disunity stand in sharp contrast to those of China's unity. From time to time*

---

35   Will Durant, in The Age of Faith (1950), marks this as the close of the Middle Ages in Europe. 1082.
36   Michael Bosworth, *The Rise and Fall of Chinese Seapower,* (1999)

the Chinese court decided to halt other activities besides overseas navigation: it abandoned development of an elaborate water-driven spinning machine, stepped back from the verge of an industrial revolution in the fourteenth century, demolished or virtually demolished mechanical clocks after leading the world in clock construction, and retreated from mechanical devices and technology in general after the late fifteenth century. The potentially harmful effects of unity have flared up again in modern China, notably in the madness of the Cultural Revolution in the 1960s and 1970s, when a decision by one or a few leaders closed the whole country's school system for five years."[37]

Europe was far from monolithic in leadership, so no one leader could exert such power. The likely innovators—the people actually doing the jobs, the engineers, the technologists, and the scholars— were almost all in the private sector, marching to the drum of self-interest. Governments could help or hinder them, but they couldn't stop them.

Back to the European Trail

By the sixteenth century commerce was growing and technology was spreading. With better sailing ships and navigation, long-distance trade was becoming commonplace. "How-To" books were being written by engineers for engineers.[38] Logarithms were invented in 1595 and, based on their principle, the slide rule in 1621.[39] The slide rule remained the primary computing tool for engineers and scientists for three hundred and fifty years, until replaced by the electronic calculator within this author's lifetime.

Armed with hindsight, we can see in the seventeenth century the leading edges of the modern world. A capitalist class had

---

37   Jared Diamond, *Guns, Germs, and Steel: The Fates of Human Societies,* (1999), 413.
38   Mokyr (1990), 64.
39   Logarithms were developed by the Scottish mathematician John Napier; the slide rule by William Oughtred, the Rector of Albany in England.

developed. Long distance trade and entrepreneurial banking offered the potential for big returns on investment for a few, and the general practice of primogeniture kept wealth from being diluted among multiple heirs at each generation. Nothing happens without capital, and for another century the primary source of capital would be individuals who had accumulated some wealth, sometimes organized into entrepreneurial groups.

The still new middle class was also expanding. The growing private sector brought increasing pressure to codify their rights to own and control their own land and property. Throughout history, and unfortunately still today, property rights have been vulnerable to the policies and the whims of leadership. In the seventeenth century Europe suffered from too many wars and from a significant economic downturn that had monarchs turning over all rocks looking for revenue. This driving need for money, as always, was in tension with the private sector that had to produce it.

In both Spain and France the resolution of this tension was controlled by the crown, to the detriment of private rights. The Dutch, though, had become the natural center of European trade, and it was commercially-minded merchants and landowners who had the influence necessary to tilt the decision; it was in their interest to protect property rights, and they did. In England the Parliament won the right to decide how to tax and to make laws, and it was also in its members' interest to guarantee property rights.

This step to secure property rights was crucially important to economic performance: property could provide collateral to obtain loans, and secure rights meant that the gains from investments were protected. In 1624 England took the first step to award innovators property rights over their innovations with a patent law.[40] This protected innovators, whose successes heretofore were

---

40   The importance of such property rights, patent laws, and the size of markets to techno-logical innovation is stressed by Douglass C North in his *Structure and Change in Economic History.* (1981) 164-166. Mokyr asserts that North overstates the case for the original British patent law, that on balance it had a positive effect but with many flaws that decreased its usefulness. Joel Mokyr, *The Enlightened Economy: An Economic History of Britain 1700-1850.* (2009), 410.

often immediately copied by others, thus benefiting the society but sometimes only marginally the innovator.

By the end of the seventeenth century Europe led the world in technical innovation, wealth, in economic vigor, and in practical, economically useful technology. Europe was dotted with waterwheels and windmills to harness the energy of every stream and breeze. The horse collar, the iron horseshoe, and the stirrup had long ago turned the horse into a very effective source of power and transportation. Continuous-flow blast furnaces and rolling mills for iron production were in operation.

Textile production largely took place at the cottage level, carried out by peasants between farm seasons using many spinning and weaving devices that had been invented to make that work more productive. The printing press was making books more easily available. There were all forms of instruments: telescopes, eye glasses, slide rules, compasses and other navigation devices, clocks of all kinds.

Over slightly more than thousand years since the dissolution of the Roman Empire there had been a definite change in the way people thought. Martin Luther's *Theses*, written and distributed in the early sixteenth century, was just part of the debate over religious issues—debate that led to the formation of the various Protestant faiths. (But it also set off a hundred or so years of terrible religious wars and atrocities as factions tried to decide whether Europe was to be Catholic or Protestant. After millions of people had died during the Thirty Years War in the first half of the seventeenth century, they settled on compromise: let people be what they wanted to be. It didn't last; states often continued to try to force conversions on people.)

Knowledge was increasingly based on observation and experiment rather than on what some ancient Greek had said. Galileo broke the ice in the early seventeenth century, when he defied ancient wisdom and the Bible by saying that the Earth was not the center of the Universe.[41] The Pope disagreed with him, and Galileo ultimately was forced to recant this heresy, but he had begun the move to put real world observation above received wisdom.

Men like Kepler, Newton, Descartes, Pascal, and Leibniz were bringing scientific thinking to the forefront of intellectual awareness. As autocracies, lay and religious, began to weaken, thoughts could be more freely expressed, and habits of rationality were strengthened.

The private sector, that had started as mostly uneducated merchants, tradesmen, and peasant farmers twelve or so centuries earlier, had now evolved to include men of learning, artists, professional of all kinds, merchants, manufacturers, and entrepreneurs—some very wealthy and influential. Peasants were still a majority, but their number was shrinking.

Particularly in England and Holland, trade had spread ideas, creating new markets and bolstering the new middle class. Improved agricultural productivity freed more people to other economic roles. The net result was that not only had the population increased, but the proportion of the population who could contribute to innovation and commercial growth had been exploding.

By the beginning of the eighteenth century the seeds of the Industrial Revolution and our modern world had been planted. It was going to happen in England.

Why England?

At the beginning of the eighteenth century England already had twice the agricultural output per worker as France, and by mid-century was ahead by four to one.[42] Only an approximate third of its population was required to feed the rest, so a much higher proportion of the population was free to do other things.

---

41   Copernicus had already advanced the heliocentric hypothesis in the sixteenth century. Galileo solidified the case.

42   Mokyr, *The Enlightened Economy*, (2009), 172.

The culminating push in the push-pull conflicts between the Parliament and the monarchy that had started five centuries earlier with the Magna Carta[43] had finally been settled, leaving England with a strong parliamentary democracy. Property rights were being strengthened, and a judiciary put in place that could enforce contracts. People were as free of restrictions as any in Europe, and had an optimistic culture and attitude. There was no social stigma attached to work; successful merchants and industrialists could gain nearly the same social status as much of the nobility.

Before the widespread adoption of the factory system, English manufacturing, with a few factories as exceptions, was done in homes and small workshops.[44] This is a wonderful environment for producing skilled tinkerers—men capable of fixing problems and spotting ways to make things work better. The English did not have as rigid a guild system as was common in much of Europe, in which qualification for membership often meant spending years learning to do something just like the master craftsman had done it all his life. There was also no not-invented-here in the British character; they were quite happy to borrow ideas from anywhere—and did.

England had joined with Scotland in 1707, at the very beginning of the eighteenth century. Scotland had less than a fifth the population of England, but supplied a surprising number of men who became prominent in the changing times.

Scottish education gets much of the credit for this. The Scots placed great emphasis on education, and the Scottish schools taught practical and scientific subjects. The Scots made substantial contribution to both Enlightenment thinking and Industrial Revolution entrepreneurship. Adam Smith, a professor at the University of Edenburgh, was a Scot.[45]

People who were not members of the Church of England were denied admittance to Oxford or Cambridge, where they would

---

43   This see-saw conflict is described in detail in Barnes, Democracy at the Crossroads, (2009).

44   Mokyr, *The Enlightened Economy*, (2009), 339.

45   Ibid, 31.

have received a classical education, learning Latin and Greek. This group, many of whom were Scots, established their own institutes of learning, the so-called "dissenting academies," modeled on the curriculum of the Scottish schools, which included a heavy dose of practical, technical, and scientific information. Quakers were also a prominent element of these nonconformists. These nonconformists were about seven percent of the population, but contributed perhaps half the entrepreneurs in manufacturing.[46]

The English worked at bridging the gap between the people who did things and the more educated people who knew things. An example is the Lunar Society, a rather loosely organized group so named because they met when the moon was full to make walking home at night easier (they called themselves 'lunatics').[47] A very substantial number of the prominent scientists and industrialists were members.

England had a middle class. Professor Mokyr noted: *"In a very poor or extremely unequal society, where the vast bulk of the population lives dangerously close to the margin of subsistence ... one would not expect a class of clockmakers or fine pottery makers to emerge. What set Britain apart was the emergence of a substantial middle class before the Industrial Revolution, a large group of merchants, professionals, well-to-do farmers, and artisan who would vaguely fall into the modern notion of a middle class."*[48]

And England had coal mines. All those coal mines demanded extraordinary effort to find ways to keep them from filling with water. The iconic innovation of the Industrial Revolution—the steam engine—had been invented to do just that. It's a fair question to ask if that first big, awkward, inefficient engine would ever have been built if English entrepreneurs hadn't been motivated by coal mines full of water.

The story goes on.

---

46 Ibid, 361.
47 The Lunar Society of Birmingham, Wikipedia, and Mokyr (2009), 56.
48 Mokyr, *The Enlightened Economy*, (2009), 116

CHAPTER 2 - THE INDUSTRIAL REVOLUTION

Agriculture was the world's first mega-innovation because it made the city possible.

The city was the second mega-innovation because it made it possible for people act and interact collectively on a large scale.

I nominate the steam engine as the world's third mega-innovation.

The steam engine was the first practical demonstration that *heat could be turned into power. The steam engine started the transition from muscle-power using energy derived from grass, oats, and hay to mechanical-power derived from coal, oil, and nuclear fission.*

This discovery made our modern world possible. It put the western world on a new trajectory of cascading innovation that would bring us the internal combustion engine, the turbine, the jet engine, and, in turn, their progeny: locomotives and railroads; steam and diesel powered ships; trucks; automobiles; airplanes; abundant electrical energy; heat-powered machinery for farming, manufacturing, and construction; air conditioning; elevators; and city streets clear of horse manure. In time, the productivity of labor would skyrocket, and with it the wealth of the common man.

The steam engine was not the only innovation in the Industrial Revolution. Everything began to change: many other technologies, the organization of the economy, the way people thought, and the theories of governance. Innovation begot innovation with accelerating fertility.

It really should have been called the Innovation Revolution.

The Steam Engine

Typical of all major innovations, the steam engine did not leap fully developed into being. It evolved through a series of progressive innovations for a hundred years before reaching the stage capable of powering a locomotive. Early in the eighteenth century, in 1712, the Englishman Thomas Newcomen built the first commercial engine to pump water out of coal mines—the large awkward device mentioned at the end of the first chapter. It was successfully used in many mines throughout England. Some half a century later, with no help whatsoever from a tea kettle, James Watt (whose name is now on every light bulb) produced the basic design of the modern steam engine.[49]

Human ingenuity is the engine of innovation, but capital is its fuel. Mr. Watt solved the need for capital by partnering with Mathew Boulton, a manufacturer whom he knew through the Lunar Society where they were both members. Mr. Boulton was able to finance the venture and his shops were equipped to manufacture the engines. The tricky job of boring the cylinders was done by John Wilkinson, who had learned the skill by boring cannon barrels.[50]

The Boulton and Watt engines became familiar all over Britain, replacing windmills and powering the factories that were beginning to supplant the cottage industries.

Engines continued to be improved, and in 1825 the world's first railroad not powered by horses was launched: the twenty-six-mile Stockton and Darlington. The project was started by a manufacturer named Edward Pease. Mr. Pease arranged the financing and obtained the necessary Parliamentary approval for his railroad. He

---

49   Wikipedia tells you more than you want to know about steam engines.

50   *Boring cannons into steam engines* is the modern version of *beating swords into plowshares.*

had originally planned on following the conventional approach of using horses for power, but was persuaded by the man who was to become his chief engineer, George Stephenson, to try a steam locomotive like Richard Trevithick had pioneered.[51] By the middle of the nineteenth century, steam was powering trains and ships all over the world. It would never be the same.

The Factory System

There were factories before the Industrial Revolution; many endeavors like iron foundries and coal mines just don't lend themselves to be cottage industries. But there weren't many. The largest industry in Britain at the time was textiles, and the producers of most textiles—and many other products—were people working at home. These were often peasant families in off-seasons, using tools designed for small production. In these cottage industries the worker had to not only produce the goods, but also take them to market—a market crowded with many just like him (or her)—to sell the finished products, and to buy the raw materials needed for the next cycle.

Not only was it a system ripe for innovation, the rapid increase in population was pushing up demand for nearly everything. The first new innovative step was a bit more specialization, in this case someone to gather up the output from a number of "cottages" and do the selling for them, and maybe buy all the needed raw materials and deliver them back to the various workers. This improved efficiency, but still left a quality control problem, best solved by having everybody work under the watchful eye of a supervisor. The next step then was to organize a factory where everybody worked under the same roof, and came to work and left at the same time everyday.

---

51   William L. Garrison and Jerry D. Ward, Tomorrow's Transportation: Changing Cities, Economies, and Lives, (2000).169-170.

Like the transition from hunting and gathering to agriculture had hugely increased total food produced, but had some real downsides for the new urban dwellers, the transition to the factory system, a transition that was to revolutionize the world with cheap and abundant products, likewise exacted a price in lives turned upside down in the process. These factory birth pains will be discussed in a later section.

The modern world would not be possible without the factory system of production. It created a leap in productivity just by reorganizing daily habits of people. But combined with the new power that came with the ability to turn heat into work and the productive machinery that was thereby enabled, western man was slated to experience a level of material abundance exceeding all imagination. The primary impact was not to be on the kings and the wealthy; the huge impact was the material wealth it was to bring to ordinary people.

And Finally—Capitalism with a Capital C

The innovative process starts with human creativity and drive—but it doesn't drive very far without capital. Nearly every entrepreneurial venture requires money. For early entrepreneurs, finding that money was a personal search. Remember, in Babylon the entrepreneur had to find the rich capitalist. In order to develop his printing press, Johannes Gutenberg borrowed from his brother-in-law. The road was sometimes bumpy, as when the brother-in-law ran out of money, and his new partner, a Mr. Fust and his son-in-law, ended up suing Mr. Gutenberg for the alleged misuse of funds.[52]

Mr. Watt, with his model of a steam engine, partnered with Mr. Boulton, who had both the manufacturing technology needed and the money. George Stephenson had been thinking "steam railroad" for a long time, and finally found Mr. Pease, who had the motivation

---

52   See *Johannes Gutenberg*, Wikipedia. Court Case.

and access to the capital. None of these capitalists were in the Yellow Pages; the entrepreneur had to find them.

With production reorganizing from the high-labor, low capital of the cottage to a much more capital-hungry factory system; with entrepreneurs wanting to build fleets of merchant ships for the Far East trade, or start another sugar cane plantation in the new world; and with increasing numbers of innovative ventures, the private sector was faced with an exploding need for capital, a need that banks could only partially fulfill.

Banks—really entrepreneurial institutions financed by wealthy individuals in partnership—had been around for a long time. The Bank of England had been established in 1694 to assemble funds to furnish loans to the government, but it was a very long time before it began to serve commercial interest and assume some of the functions of a central bank in regulating the currency.

But true banks—financed by deposits that should be redeemable at any time—can't prudently lend money for ventures where the chances of failure are high, simply because they can't afford to lose their depositors' money. Prudent banks couldn't lend money to entrepreneurs who wanted to send ships to the East Indies because they could lose it all if the venture failed, and would not share the large rewards that would come with success—at best, they would only get their money back. For risky ventures the arrangement had to be one under which the entity putting up the money—and therefore taking the risk—could also participate in the rewards.

What had been missing were institutions that could raise large amounts of capital suitable for such riskier commercial and innovative ventures. The growing size of the capital needs required reaching a very wide base of investors—anonymous investors because the needs exceeded what was possible with the personal search. Capitalism acquires a capital "C" when the institutions of *finance* are broadened to include such institutions. This system had started at the beginning of the seventeenth century.

In 1601 the Dutch East India Company had been granted monopoly powers by the Dutch government to pursue the spice trade in Asia. The company wanted to build lots of new ships for this venture, and they needed new capital. They organized in such a way that they could sell fractions of the venture to a larger number of investors, investors whom they need not know, and who need not know them. In 1602 they set up a market, the Amsterdam Stock Exchange, to sell and trade these fractions or "shares." Anybody could buy a piece of the Company, and, as part owners, share in its profits—or find themselves wiser but poorer if all the ships sank.

A stock exchange is just another kind of market; a market for fractional ownership in a commercial venture. It was introduced as a way to facilitate raising capital by broadening the base of potential ownership. As time passed, such exchanges were used to trade all kinds of financial entities.

Such a market only works if the products being traded are attractive to the customers. Here the product being traded is the ownership of companies. The customers, the people doing the buying and selling, may not know anyone in the company and will have no direct control over the company's actions. So a form of organization of the companies was needed to make ownership of its shares attractive under these impersonal conditions.

The *corporation* became the common format. It was not new; stock companies—essentially corporations—had been around for a long time. A corporation is a legal entity whose existence is not tied to the life of any real person, so it can theoretically live forever. A corporation may disappear because it failed in business, but not because somebody died. Further, the obligations it entails are its own responsibility, just as if it were a person; they are not the responsibility of its stockholders. So people who buy shares don't have to worry that they will lose their investment because people are mortal or that they would become personally liable for the corporation's losses or screw-ups.

It's easy to underestimate the importance of the corporate form of business organization. Here was the world moving into a new phase: large factories starting to replace cottage industries, growing population indulging in commerce on an unprecedented scale, and all needing more capital than could be put together by any reasonably-sized group of partners using their own money. Invention is not necessarily cheap, but the step to convert it into widespread use, the innovative step, almost always requires a heavy investment; abundant capital is a critical requirement to support widespread innovation. *The corporate form of organization and a public market for its ownership made it possible to raise capital in the quantities needed in this budding new world. Without it, the scale of endeavor would have been severely limited and potential economic expansion constrained.* [53]

By the early eighteenth century there were stock exchanges in France, England, and Holland. Near the end of that century, in 1792, twenty-four brokers sitting under a buttonwood tree at 68 Wall Street signed the Buttonwood Agreement that was the start of the New York Stock Exchange here in the then very new United States.

It is very easy to overlook the central importance of banking and stock trading to the evolution of wealth. The modern financial system is a mechanism that allows capital from a very large number of sources to be funneled into the growth of the economy. Further, the capital is funneled selectively: each investor decides where he wants to put his money. Thus investors collectively decide through their individual choices how the capital will be allocated to generate the most wealth. The process also helps the possessor of otherwise idle capital; money is useless under a mattress. The genius of the financial system that has evolved is that it allows the entrepreneur

---

53   As an aside, Islamic law lacks a concept of legal personhood, which is essential to the concept of a corporation. That, plus the Islamic inheritance system that required an equal distribution of an estate to all children, inhibited the accumulation of capital in substantial amounts. Both are a real inhibition to large scale innovation and commercial enterprise. Landes, Chap 3 by Timur Kuran, *"The Scale of Entrepreneurship in Middle Eastern History: Inhibitive Roles of Islamic Institutions."* (2010), Kindle Locations 2230-2250.

to be paired with people with money *without either knowing the other.*

New Thinking

Historians also refer to the eighteenth century as the Age of Enlightenment or the Age of Reason. At its core was a critical questioning of traditional institutions, customs, and morals, and a strong belief in rationality and science. New societal values like personal freedom and radical ideas of representative government were taking shape. The Constitution of the new United States of America started with the words *"We the People"*; that was a revolution in a world accustomed to kings and *"l'Etat est moi"*.[54]

People throughout the western world increasingly enjoyed greater personal freedom, the right to own property, and to benefit from their own accomplishments—all those conditions that would improve the climate for the technological creativity so central to the growth of wealth over time.

Mankind is creative. Whether that creativity gets expressed to society's betterment depends on the conditions under which he lives. The new ideas of culture and governance that sprang from the Enlightenment greatly favored innovative behavior, and therefore did much to shape the world we live in today.

I Nominate 1776

Historians say the Industrial Revolution began between 1750 and 1830. The new financial systems geared to broadening the base of capital creation were also getting traction in this same period. Picking a specific date for the start of these transitions will not change any reality, but it satisfies people who want a start date, however arbitrary

If a date is to be picked, I nominate 1776.

---

54   "I am the state." Attributed to Louis XIV of France.

In 1776 the first Boulton and Watt steam engine was delivered to a customer.

1776 was the year that the Scottish Professor Adam Smith published *An Inquiry into the Nature and Causes of the Wealth of Nations*, which many class as the most influential book on economic behavior ever written. Professor Smith argued that it was the self-interested pursuit of gain that produced benefit to the society at large: "*It is not from the benevolence of the butcher, the brewer, or the baker, that we expect our dinner, but from their regard to their own self-interest.*" He reasoned that each person, by following his own self-interest, without direction from anyone else, produced a coherent and balanced economy "*as if guided by an invisible hand.*" He described in detail the economic benefits of the division of labor. He was a realist: he recognized clearly that men are somewhat less than perfect, and some controls were necessary to further justice and morality.

In 1776 stock exchanges were common in Europe, and were to have their advent on the west side of the ocean in another 16 years.

Last, in 1776 the birth of a new nation was announced, an experiment in governance *by the people*, a nation that was to become preeminent in the development and demonstration of the strength of capitalism as a hospitable economic climate for innovation and wealth creation.

Birth Pains

In the one hundred and fifty years from 1700 to 1850, the population of England increased from 5.3 million to 15.9 million people. In 1700, 17 percent lived in towns over five thousand in population; in 1850 that had risen to 45 percent. So urban population increased from about 900 thousand to 7.2 million people in one hundred and fifty years. Almost half of this change was in the last fifty years, the first half of the nineteenth century.[55]

---

55   Mokyr, *The Enlightened Economy*, (2009) 281,456

Why did people come to the cities? First, the factories were replacing the cottage industries, so the cottage workers could no longer make a living in the countryside. Contrary to a common assumption, there was no significant decrease in the need for farm labor that also forced these folks into the cities. It is true that agricultural farm labor productivity was increasing rapidly,[56] but so was the population that had to be fed. Higher wages in the cities also lured people (that gain was illusory because of higher living costs in the cities). And a few farsighted folks could see that in spite of current conditions, the future was in the cities, not the countryside.

It was a time of wrenching change for many people. The rural life with its cottage industries permitted great flexibility in daily life, so the family could set their own schedules and modes of work. They were accustomed to the intimate culture of the small village. As urban factory workers they lost their old more relaxed life and had to learn to keep a schedule, and to interact with a boss and with fellow workers. And there was no joy in urban living compared to the rural life.

Cities couldn't stay ahead of the influx of new people. Already dense because they were designed around walking, it was hard to supply enough housing to keep up with the growing urban population. In the more rapidly growing industrial centers the problem was especially acute for the new, unskilled and very low-wage factory workers: whole families to a room, no running water, no sewage disposal, no heating, inadequate security—industrial slums. This resulted in terribly unhealthy conditions and badly deteriorating social behavior.

Inadequate nutrition and ever-present disease were no help. Life expectancy in the 1850's gives a clue: it was estimated at 31-32 years in the worst industrial cities of Manchester and Liverpool, 38 years in London, and the national average was 41 years.[57]

---

56   The enclosure movement contributed to this. With open field agriculture small, individual, often scattered plots were unfenced, and reverted to commons after harvest. It was more efficient to make much larger plots and fence them.

57   Mokyr, *The Enlightened Economy*, (2009) 299

William Blake (1757–1827), a man whose poems and sayings take up over four pages in Bartlett's *Familiar Quotations*, coined the phrase "dark Satanic mills." He used it in a poem about John Milton, so it's dubious that he was talking about a factory, but it has caught on in that context. Charles Dickens brought this dark side of the nineteenth century in England to life in his novels.

People had not learned how to cope with the rapid change this new world was creating. The economic and social doctrine of the day led to acceptance that these awful conditions were just the way the world was supposed to be. A few protests that had gotten out of hand had led less toward sympathy for the plight of this new industrial working class than fear of them. The general diagnosis was that moral depravity caused poverty; it took many decades for that diagnosis to change enough to consider that such terrible poverty might cause moral depravity.

The church didn't help. Its sermons focused on "it's your fault, now do better!" The not-surprising result was for many to abandon religion altogether.

Slowly it was recognized that something had to be done. While economic growth was booming, the awful penalty on the urban industrial poor had finally attracted some sympathy, and some recognition that this was a serious societal problem.

Initially the government only treated symptoms. In the Factory Act of 1802 Parliament began by regulating child labor: children couldn't work in textile factories more than 12 hours a day. The Act of 1819 restricted employment until they were at least nine years old, and were restricted to eight hours per day until they were over thirteen. Over time, laws to improve other aspects of working conditions were passed. These laws were widely evaded.[58] There were further Acts in 1833, 1842, and 1847; slowly they began to bite.

The basic cause of these ills, though, was finally diagnosed—rightly or wrongly—as inadequate bargaining power on the part of

---

58   Ibid 335-336

the working person: they had no leverage with their employers, no political power, and no access to sources of help. The prescription was to legalize the right to organize into labor unions. (England did not have rigid guilds.) By 1868 114 thousand workers were unionized in England. Over the next twenty-six years, that grew to 1.5 million.

The very astute and able British economist Alfred Marshall offered an alternate analysis. He blamed low pay on low productivity. He had spent many, many hours in factories in both England and America studying their operation in great detail. He observed that competition forced factory owners to continually push for better productivity by incrementally introducing new technology and more efficient behavior and organization. He also observed that as productivity rose, so did wages. [59] His analysis was correct, but people with very low productivity still had to live.

Later in the century the problem of the urban industrial poor was no longer seen as a matter of moral deficiency but as an economic problem. People began to accept the view that a modern industrial nation needed a work force that was well-fed, well-educated, socially integrated, and potentially innovative. Action had to be taken as necessary to prevent any recurrence of conditions such as those that had prevailed in the early days of the new factory system.[60]

The second consequence of this grim experience with early factories was the serious elevation of the socialist idea and ideal. The first volume of Karl Marx's *Das Kapital* was published in 1867. This socialist ideal, implemented in real nations, has cost millions of people the material well-being that a well-regulated capitalist system could have supplied. Worse, the ruthless dictatorships that arose under the socialist banner have cost the world multimillions of lives.

---

59   Sylvia Nasar, Grand Pursuit: The Story of Economic Genius. (2011) Kindle location 1290-97.

60   This account leans heavily on Bartlett, The Development of European Civilization, Lectures 25-32, (2011). The author accepts responsibility for its interpretation.

Nineteenth Century Innovation

By the nineteenth century the wave of eighteenth century technological innovation had become a flood. No ancient emperor or great conqueror, or any modern ruler, could have had nearly the impact on the world had by the men causing and exploiting this innovation.

Until the nineteenth century all large cities had developed very near some body of water simply because transportation on land was terrible: roads were hard to maintain, and speeds were limited to how fast the horse could carry or pull its load. The railroad changed all that. The steam-powered locomotive and railroads let cities locate away from water and let them be fed from distant farmlands. By the end of the century there were over one hundred and fifty thousand miles of railroad track integrating the United States.

The steam ship with screw propellers magnified international trade, the steam-powered factory greatly improved productivity, and, by the end of the century, steam-supplied electricity was transforming everything. The Bessemer furnace, introduced in mid-nineteenth century, increased the output of steel needed to make railroad tracks—and many other things.

The Briton Isambard Kingdom Brunel (1806-1859) was probably the best engineer in the world at the time. He started as a very successful bridge designer; he designed and built a tunnel under the Thames, the first in the world under a navigable river; and he invented the screw propeller and designed the first all-steam, iron-hulled vessel without side-wheel paddles. His Great Eastern was the largest ship in the world at that time, and could go nonstop from England to Australia.

When the Stockton and Darlington railroad was moving people and cargo at ten to fifteen miles per hour, Brunel designed and built the Great Western Railroad, upon which trains cruised at sixty miles per hour. He pulled this off by using a 7 foot gauge (distance between the rails) rather than the 4 foot 8.5 inches used on the Stockton and Darlington. This allowed larger wheels without getting too tippy, and larger wheels produced greater speed at the same rate of turning. Brunel's system was much more expensive, largely because the higher speed required straighter track, which required digging through hills rather than going around them.

In 1844 Parliament set up a committee to decide whether the standard for the nation should be 4 foot 8.5 inches or 7 feet; it chose the 4 foot 8.5 inch standard because it was cheaper to build and because so much of the smaller gauge had already been built.[61] (The 4 foot 8.5 inch gauge is still used almost everywhere in the world, the legacy of a now ancient committee meeting. Try to imagine what trains might look like today if the decision had gone to support the 7 foot gauge.)

Introduced in mid-century, the first urban trolleys, riding on rails, were horse-drawn. In the last part of the century electric motors replaced the horses. These trolleys let cities expand into "trolley suburbs", relieving some of the terrible crowding and congestion. Workers no longer had to live next to the factories where they worked. London had the first urban transportation system to be put underground.

In 1837 Samuel Morse's telegraph provided the first communication that did not depend on transportation, and forty years later the Brunel-designed Great Eastern steam ship was used to lay telegraph cables across the Atlantic. Now the time required for someone in New York to question someone in London and get an answer dropped from thirty days to closer to thirty minutes. The new innovations in transportation and communication shrank the world.

The internal combustion engine was a product of that century, but its impact was delayed until the Ford Model T in the early twentieth. Then the invention of asphalt[62] early in the nineteenth

---

61   Garrison and Ward, *Tomorrow's Transportation*, (2000) 175
62   The Macadam road was made from a mixture of stone aggregate and tar developed by John MacAdam, a Scot. Hence the name 'tarmac' often used today.

century permitted a veritable explosion of good roads in the twentieth.

The automobile and the truck spelled the end of horses in our cities. In the late nineteenth and early twentieth centuries, horses were the motive power for almost everything that moved. It is estimated that there were some 90,000 horses working in New York in the 1880's. These horses left nearly a thousand tons of manure on the streets every day, and 15 thousand carcasses every year.[63] The effluent of the cars and trucks that replaced them certainly had their downside, but it was less obvious than that of the horse.

The steam engine and the internal combustion engine were in the process of changing horses and sails from two of the western world's more important sources of power and transportation to two of its more expensive hobbies.

Whereas pragmatic tinkering had been the source of innovation for almost all of history, by the nineteenth century, and increasingly in the twentieth, science was becoming the source of ideas driving much if not most of modern innovation. Science was moving from being an interesting hobby to an activity with economic worth.

Raising More Capital

The pace of innovation was exploding in early twentieth century, and innovation requires capital. Stock exchanges were a source once a company had been formed to carry an innovation forward, but it was no help in the very early stages of incubation. This gap was sometimes filled by individuals with a high net worth who were willing to accept the very high risks of betting on ideas and invention still in garages for the potentially huge returns coming from the few that succeeded. These folks came to be called "angel" investors, a modern and wealthier version, perhaps, of Gutenberg's brother-in-law.

---

63   Joel Tarr, Urban Pollution: Many Long Years Ago. *American Heritage* XXII, (Oct. 1971)

After WW II ended, a new kind of organization was introduced in the United States specifically to help innovative ventures in their early incubation stages. These so-called Venture Capital organizations would provide technical and managerial assistance as well as capital, and typically would cash-out when the venture was sufficiently advanced to become an Initial Public Offering on a stock exchange. There are now a multitude of these Venture Capital organizations, all actively searching for and evaluating new innovative possibilities.

The competition for capital is fierce. The individuals and organizations that are doing the investing make the choices that allocate the capital. If investors think Corporation X is going to prosper they buy larger amounts of that stock, which increases its price on the stock exchange. The higher price of the stock and the willingness of investors to buy more makes it easy for the company to raise more capital by selling more stock. If investors are less impressed, then the price of the stock falls, and the company finds it can't sell more stock without driving the price still lower, obviously constraining the ability to raise capital. So the stock exchange has become an allocation device as well as a capital-raising device.

Our stock exchanges are often treated as a substitute for a casino, but it is the very fact of this speculation that makes them an allocation device: people bet on the best prospects for gain. Nor does this speculation prevent stock exchanges from being a real source of capital for business and entrepreneurship. The stock market also provides an investment option that allows the general public to passively participate in the wealth generation of the economy.

It is perfectly obvious that the financial system that has evolved is complex, and its purposes sometimes obscure. And, judging from recent turmoil, a bit more evolution seems like a good idea. *But capitalism—a free market plus a financial system to provide and allocate the capital that enables commerce and innovation—is the only system the world knows that truly provides a climate and a financial mechanism for the imagination of human minds to be translated into reality.* Growth and improvement come from the latter act; capitalism only supports its realization.

Economic organizations innovate to accommodate both changing scale and new technology. The factory organization replaced the cottage. We have already told the story of the Dutch East India Company and the Amsterdam Stock Exchange, which was the organizational response to better ship technology and attractive, distant markets. The innovation of the steam locomotive introduced the need for new kinds of organizations to build and operate railroads. The airlines of the twentieth century did not invent the airplane; the airplane motivated the invention of the airlines.

So the private sector finds itself in an almost continuous state of organizational flux as it adapts to new technical innovations and changing markets. The culture exploits and evolves.

Before the mass-produced automobile it's doubtful that most people had been more than fifty miles from where they were born. The automobile changed that. It enabled the reshaping of our cities by making large suburbs practical. The airplane revolutionized long-range transportation; we now routinely eat grapes from Chile and visit the pyramids on a two-week vacation. In mid-twentieth century the shipping container revolutionized freight transportation. The contraceptive pill made women masters of their own lives. The discovery of DNA is in the process of enabling the development of drugs that are tailored to both the person and the disease. Computers, cell phones, and the internet—we really don't know where that is leading society. Significant breakthroughs have occurred in every branch of science that we know of; all these are being exploited in ways that affect our economy, our culture, our governance—our lives.

Not all has been rosy. The evolutionary road has been punctuated with painful potholes: economic downturns and recessions and depressions that we still do not know how to prevent. Worse, bad patches in the evolutionary road have motivated concepts of governance that have done terrible damage to the world by failing to provide adequate standards of living, and by providing fertile ground for terrible men to sow destruction.

Socialism

One of the innovations of the nineteenth century was socialism, largely conceived in response to the birth pains of the factory system of production. The fundamental idea in its purest form was to cut off the invisible hand at the wrist, and put all production and distribution decisions in the very visible hands of central planners. It was and is an idea for running a society that is appealing to many—more in the past than today.

It hasn't worked out in practice quite the way its advocates hoped and advertised. Socialism has come to mean state-dominated. The old Soviet Union and the old China under Mao are real-life examples. Cuba and North Korea are still on the list, as were, until recently, some east European countries.

In such state-dominated countries nearly every important decision was made by a central authority. Any significant property was state-controlled. Planners decided what was to be produced, how it was to be produced, and who was to get the output. Prices— mostly guesses—were set by the central planners, not by balancing actual supply and demand. But rather than a benign authority, trying to achieve *"from each according to his ability and to each according to his need,"* these planners were very much under the thumb of dictators who had their own agendas. The vast majority of the populace were essentially automatons, working at the jobs they are assigned, with no freedom to pursue their own interests. They did achieve equality: everyone except for the governing elite enjoyed roughly the same level of misery.[64]

These state-dominated nations have offered no contest in economic performance compared to capitalism. All of the old and

---

[64] "the same level of misery" is borrowed fron an observation attributed to Sir Winston Churchill.

stable western nations have citizens with a high degree of personal freedom with rights protected by law; these are now rich by any historical standard, while no centrally planned nation had lifted the majority of their citizens past our definition of poverty.

Why has free-market capitalism won so resoundingly? There are two primary reasons. First, the incentives under socialism are not designed to bring forth peoples' best efforts. People are not working for their own interests; they do what they are told to do, and their reward, their pay, is little affected by how well they do it. There was a phrase attributed to the old Soviet worker: "We pretend to work, and they pretend to pay us."

The second reason is because better economic decisions are made in the free society. This is not an allusion to the intelligence of socialist planners, but to the quality and timeliness of the information with which they have to make decisions. State planners can never collect all the information that is spread throughout the private sector. They can't know all the details: how do central planners decide how many sushi restaurants are needed in Bishop, California, or how many green shirts, size 14-32, are needed in Biloxi, Mississippi? Since the price system is artificial, not set by supply and demand, the planner is without prices or price trends to signal shortages or excesses. Further, the state planner is also subject to autocratic whim.[65]

Under capitalism, economic decisions are largely made by the people who are closest to and have the most intimate knowledge of the matter at hand, and have the personal motivation to make those decisions as best they know how. They have the advantage of real prices that have been set in the market, signaling what is happening to supply and demand throughout that sector of the economy. (The impact of government regulations on this decision process is discussed in Chapter 4.)

---

65 Friedrich Hayek, an Austrian economist, was prominent in analyzing the role of information in economic decision making. For example, see The Use of Knowledge in Society, reprinted in Wikipedia from the *American Economic Review, XXXV*, No. 4, (September, 1945), 519-530.

Added to the information dearth, there are two other missing ingredients in the state-dominated model: the right to own and control private property and the freedom to exercise one's own initiative for one's own benefit.

There are moral arguments for freedom, which will be left to others to put forward. But the superiority of capitalism as an economic system is obviously recognized: in the last thirty years China, the Soviet Union, and many other nations have been lured by the success of capitalism to move in the direction of a capitalistic system. Most have a long way to go, but the reality of the failure of the state-dominated economic system became so stark that it cried out for change. Socialism—state domination—has clearly lost the luster it had earlier in the century.

The luster has dulled, but it hasn't disappeared. The responsibility to care for ourselves in a capitalist economy is always in competition with the memory of having our parents doing things for us, and leads many to think that some degree of socialism, with the state doing the worrying about some of aspects of life, might be a warmer and more comfortable world. Nations do try to find a compromise, a middle way, a way to shift more personal responsibility to the government without jeopardizing the benefits of free market capitalism.

Since all goods and services are produced by the private sector, anything the government does to supply services to the populace requires that it take the funds from the private sector: there is no other source. To the degree these extracted funds reduce investment, the state-supplied service penalizes growth; to the degree these extracted funds reduce consumption, the state-supplied service reduces the standard of living of the non-recipients of the service. Further, unless the government can supply the service as efficiently as the people would have supplied it for themselves, there is a net loss. It seems almost inevitable that shifting a service from individuals to the state will result in slower growth and some living-standard penalty to at least the non-recipients of that service.

Capitalism Today

Capitalism is ideally an economic system in which free minds operating in a free market are supported by a financial system design to raise and allocate capital.

Under ideal capitalism individuals have property rights protected by law, and are free to decide what they want to do with their own talent and labor; each is free to own and control property, to operate a business for profit, to trade their labor for a wage, to save, to borrow from a willing lender, to invest, or to try something new. Each individual makes the primary economic decisions relative to his or her own situation.

These individual and independent decisions determine the overall direction and performance of the total economy. Within the bounds of regulatory constraint, there is no need for authoritarian guidance; the coherence and efficiency of the economy illustrates the efficacy of Adam Smith's "invisible hand." The very notion that an economy guided only by people pursuing their own self-interests in their own way could be superior to one guided by planners is probably the hardest concept for most people to grasp.

The decisions to organize stock exchanges and the other institutions designed to raise and allocate capital came from the actions of these individuals acting in their own interest; they, too, were designed by the invisible hand, not imposed by some authority.

The market determines who gets the goods and services generated, not some planner, committee of judges, or roll of dice.

Whether or not an investment is to be successful is determined entirely by the voluntary reaction of its customers or users, not by some arbitrary authority. People get only what other people are willing to pay for their labor or output.

The complicating factor is that there is no such thing as this "pure" capitalism: all so-called capitalistic nations are hybrids, a mixture of free-market and government participation. As will be discussed in Chapter 4, The Role and Impact of Government, even "ideal" capitalism needs some government. But too much can be the enemy, and its optimum role is a fiercely argued matter.

This nation started with and has retained a national culture clearly receptive to and supportive of innovation, with entrepreneurs to produce, and investors to finance. We should enjoy reasonable confidence in our economic future, but we do not. Capitalism is not understood by far too many. Many object to its sharp edges, and its survival as a healthy system is not guaranteed. The rest of this book is aimed at illuminating and analyzing these issues.

PART II

FUTURE EVOLUTION: WHERE DO WE GO FROM HERE?

CHAPTER 3 - SHARP EDGES

The United States a century ago looked like a third world country. Out of a hundred American homes two had electricity, maybe ten had flush toilets, some fourteen had bathtubs, and about twenty or so had running water. None had refrigerators, washing machines, or air conditioning, and only a few had central heating. Most cities were just then in the process of installing sewer systems hooked up to homes. Maternal mortality was some somewhere between sixty and one hundred times worse than today,[66] and real wages in manufacturing had only one-forth the real buying power of today's wages.[67]

In roughly four generations the compounding of innovation in our free-market capitalistic system has brought us to the material well-being of our lives today. One would think that capitalism would therefore be widely, even wildly, popular. It is not. Unfortunately, capitalism and the innovation it fosters have some downsides that are joined at the hip to its success. It also gets a bit of gratuitous blame that it doesn't earn.

---

66   *Maternal Deaths*, Wikipedia.
67   Mostly from Wattenberg, The First Measured Century, (2001), and *The Free Dictionary*, Wikipedia.

Turnover in the Job Market

Innovation is heartless; the new pushes out the old. Slightly over a century ago over a third of the labor force of the country was still on farms; now it is something like two percent. This has forced a dramatic reorientation of millions of lives, all because the internal combustion engine replaced the horse, and better fertilizers and seeds have revolutionized farm productivity. The invention of the automobile killed the need for buggy whips, so the workers in the buggy whip factory had to find new work. Nobody shovels horse manure out of streets any more.[68]

The same thing that happened to the agricultural sector is now happening in manufacturing. In the last forty years manufacturing output more than doubled, but the proportion of the labor force in manufacturing has dropped from about 26 percent to 9 percent.[69] As was the case in agriculture, lots of people have had to find new jobs.

Our material wealth today comes from both improved productivity and wider capabilities. Improved productivity means it takes fewer people to produce the same output. Wider capability derives from new inventions that allow people do things they couldn't do before. Both result from innovation, and part of the price is job turnover. We have not found a way to escape this tradeoff.

Overall, there have been far more job gains than job losses— enough to both replace those lost to innovation and to match the job needs of our rising population. Many, maybe most, people are now working at jobs that didn't exist fifty years ago, or in jobs that have changed so radically that they would be hard to recognize.

---

68   Until the twentieth century almost all horsepower that powered transportation in cities was provided by horses.

69   Data from Perry, U.S. Manufacturing: More Output from Fewer Workers, (2009) in *Seeking Alpha*.

But when Joe loses his job because of some innovation, he may know that in the long run everybody will be better off, but in the short run he still doesn't have a job.

Governments have tried to fight the inevitable by making it hard to lay off employees. Companies respond by being very slow to rehire.

Labor unions have sometimes been successful in negotiating labor agreements that constrain management's ability to lay off excess workers, thus nullifying the prospect of lower prices and higher sales. This seems to work well until competition puts the company in jeopardy. General Motors, Ford, and Chrysler might be able to comment on this.

Policies and actions that facilitate easier job switching are sensible. Better and broader education to improve flexibility would seem to be useful, but education can only go so far; welders don't turn easily into software architects. The job losses may be in Chicago and the new jobs in Denver. If there are silver bullets, we haven't found them.

There is a concern that, unlike the past, we will not generate enough new jobs to absorb all those that are being lost to improving productivity. This concern has been with us for at least some two hundred years, but has so far been unfounded. But it is a rational concern, because robots and other forms of flexible automation are replacing jobs, and will do so in the future at an even greater rate. Appendix A discusses the issue in slightly more depth.

Unequal Rewards

The free-market process does not reward people equally. This should not come as a surprise: people are not equal. They are born with different mental equipment, different levels of health and energy, acquire different levels of education, have different interests and goals and different levels of inherent motivation to reach those goals, and enjoy different levels of luck. Under the capitalistic system, the size of the slice that accrues to each is a result of how all those factors combine. There is no way that these slices will be equal.

Income inequality among households has been increasing. This change has been exaggerated by the very rapidly rising incomes in just the small sliver of households at the top, which, between 1979 and 2007, rose by 275 percent. The other 19 percent in the top 20 rose by 65 percent [70], while the bottom 20 percent rose by only 28 percent.[71] That top 1 percent is not always the same households; someone gets a windfall, makes the top 1 percent that year, and the next year that household is back down in the pack.

There are logical reasons for this growing inequality. The world is becoming much more technically complex. This has placed an increasing premium on the labor of those few who have invested in the education necessary to cope with this complexity, and the even smaller number who are the prime innovators in this very technical world. These innovators are well represented in the top 1 percent of incomes.

It is also logical that so much growth has occurred in just the top 1 percent sliver of people and their households. Better communication and video capabilities have allowed entertainers and sports figures to reach very much larger audiences than in the past, so their economic worth for advertising has increased accordingly. The very best of these—the ones that really draw the audiences—earn fabulous compensation.

Many of our large corporations operate all around the world and have to deal with increasingly complicated political issues and conflicting regulations and pressures. The decisions made by the leaders of these companies influence literally billions of dollars and thousands of lives, one way or another. The bidding for the few people with the skill and temperament to manage these companies has driven their compensation to higher and higher levels. Most

---

70   James Pethekoukis, Oct 26, 2011, *7 Reasons Why Obama Is Wrong About Inequality*, The Enterprise Blog using CBO data.
71   *Income Inequality in the United States*, Wikipedia

company executives receive a large part of their compensation in stock, so that if their companies thrive and the stock rises their gains can be truly impressive. Steve Jobs and Bill Gates were groundbreaking entrepreneurs who innovated, from the ground up, things of considerable worth to us all, and they prospered enormously as the companies they built grew.

Some people resent the pay of business executives because they view large companies as mostly rapacious, thinking only of profit, with little regard for people or social good. There probably is no cure for that perception, but it might be tempered a bit by just a modicum of understanding of how the economy works. Successful business leaders have done much more to improve our material lives than has any government or political figure. Steve Jobs' and Bill Gates' stories are analogous to those of Carnegie, who built our steel industry, and Rockefeller our oil industry: their products, at prices much lower than they had ever been, greatly enriched the nation. They built the companies that did this and they became extremely rich. (As an aside, they also invented truly muscular philanthropy.)

The inequality that exists today is exaggerated by the fact that the comparison usually stops with a comparison of household incomes. The inequality is impressive: in 2010 the top 20 percent of households had over fifteen times the income of the bottom 20 percent. Now that is inequality! It is also very misleading.

In 2010 there were 1.97 earners on average in the households in the top 20 percent (more married couples), and 0.42 earners in the bottom 20 percent (more single parents and unemployed people). This implies that in the top 20 percent there were almost two people working to earn the household income, while in the bottom 20 percent households only 42 percent had someone in them who was earning money. So if instead of comparing households we compare earners that fifteen shrinks to a factor of a little over three, not nearly as impressive.[72]

---

72   Mark J. Perry, Oct 21, 2011, *Income Inequality can be explained by Household Demographics*, The Enterprise Blog, using CBO data.

Inequality in accumulated wealth—the size of assets owned—is much greater than the inequality in annual incomes. In the United States 34 percent of wealth is held by the top 1 percent and 84 percent by the top 20 percent of folks. The rationale for that huge disparity is simple: the magic of compounding. The economy has generally grown over time, and assets invested in the economy have grown with it. Prudence, patience, compounded growth, and sometimes a bit of luck can let small assets grow into big assets, and big assets into great wealth. Most people never accumulate any assets to get started on that road.

The picture is sometimes exaggerated. The press is fond of showing how the people in the bottom X percent bracket are so much worse off than the people in the top bracket. Such data is always good for a polemic or two. The use of household data without correcting for demographic trends is one type of distortion. There are others.

Few people have ever heard the story of Hypothetistan. In Hypothetistan everyone was equal: everybody went to work at age twenty, retired at sixty-five, and all earned exactly the same amounts over their lifetimes. Everybody worked hard, took advantage of all opportunities to advance their skills and educations, so their salaries at age sixty-five were ten times bigger than the sorry pay they got when they started at age twenty. The statistics, of course, clearly showed that the bottom 10 percent of earners (which would naturally be the younger workers) made almost ten times less than the top 10 percent of earners (who, of course, were the older workers).

Things did not go well in Hypothetistan. An enterprising young reporter saw these statistics, and immediately wrote a story about how unfair it was that some people made ten times as much as other people. The people cried "Do something!" so the government did something: it taxed away anything people made over the average wage, and gave it to people earning less than the average wage. Now everybody got the same amount of money every payday. The young people wondered why they should work so hard when they were going the get the same amount of money anyway, and the older people wondered why they should work so hard when they weren't going to get to keep much of their money anyway.

I suspect this is why no one has ever heard of Hypothetistan.

The moral of the story is obvious: statistics comparing the bottom X percent of earners with the top X percent of earners can be very misleading because people don't stay in the same brackets over time. It suggests one shouldn't draw any conclusions from this kind of data. Comparing the earnings of all thirty-year-olds or all fifty- year-olds or some other age would be more enlightening.

Even though objections to inequality may partly rest on misperceptions, it is hard not to conclude that it has become a serious issue. Many want to achieve greater equality of result through income transfer. One should differentiate between income transfer as needed to maintain a social safety net for those in temporary difficulties, and income transfer to equalize incomes. These have very different impacts on society. The latter has a pernicious effect on motivations that is dangerous to the society. It demotivates both the recipient and the contributor. It assumes that the rewards earned by very successful people can be confiscated without loss of their talents and effort, and that the bounty transferred to the less hardworking or successful to achieve equality will not affect the efforts of these recipients.

The following quote is from Will and Ariel Durant in their book, *The Lessons of History*:[73] *"Utopias of equality are biologically doomed, and the best that the amiable philosopher can hope for is an approximate equality of justice and educational opportunity. A society in which all potential abilities are allowed to develop and function will have a survival advantage in the competition of groups."*

---

73   Will and Ariel Durant, *The Lessons of History*, (1968), 23.

Attitudes Toward Wall Street

Many people have a mistrust bordering on animosity toward Wall Street and the large investment banks that seem to dominate it. They blame it for the subprime fiasco and the recession that resulted. The bailouts the government supplied to banks and other companies when the housing bubble burst are resented. The well-advertised high salaries and large bonuses in the financial industry only rub salt into the wounds.

Some—but certainly not all—of this bitterness toward Wall Street as a cause of the subprime recession is misplaced; some of the institutions did play a high-risk game. But Wall Street did not cause the subprime crisis, the government did. The already extant practices in the private sector added fuel, but the fire had been started by the government's willingness to abrogate economic reality.

Business people do not voluntarily lend to people if there is high risk they will not be repaid, but for two decades the government mandated that banks must lend to marginal borrowers.[74] The lending institutions did not resist this mandate because the government arranged to remove the risk of these dubious loans by purchasing them through the government-sponsored enterprises, Fannie May and Freddie Mac. In fact, some of lenders actively encouraged the scheme because, with the taxpayer assuming the risk, making subprime loans was profitable.

After the bubble burst, the government was quite successful in deflecting the attention from their own culpability in precipitating the sub prime disaster onto Wall Street.[75]

While the subprime crisis is the most immediate sore spot in the public eye, Wall Street does have structural problems. There is concern that the large investment banks have been too successful, that their efforts to make money is both increasing their

---

74   The Community Reinvestment Act of 1977, strengthened in 1992.

75   The message of the 2009 movie *Capitalism: A Love Story* was not significantly different from that coming from some members of Congress. Wall Street was front and center.

vulnerability to failure and at the same time making them so large that their failure could damage the whole economy. The five largest banks now control 61 percent of the nation's commercial banking assets, up from 26 percent twenty years ago. The concern is that these few have become too big to fail, and therefore will essentially force the government to bail them again in the next crisis.[76] This knowledge, in itself, reduces the motivation for prudence. Here is an area where some purposeful evolution is badly needed.[77]

The nation needs Wall Street, warts and all. As was described earlier, stock exchanges were started to provide a market for the trade of ownership in companies to raise and allocate capital. There are now various exchanges in place to serve other functions: to trade futures and options that allow actions to be temporized or shifted in time; to trade financial instruments that embody various forms of insurance to let risk be shifted from one entity to another; and to trade in the bonds issued by both the government and by private sector companies. In essence, markets now trade in ownership, debt, time shifting, and risk. The smooth functioning of these exchanges and the banking system are crucial to national economic health.

The sheer complexity of this modern system makes it opaque. To many, even without Wall Street getting more than its share of the stigma of the subprime recession, our stock exchanges look like a huge casino, one that seems to happily take advantage of ordinary people by helping them lose their money. This perception is unfortunate, because Wall Street is the symbol of capitalism, and capitalism doesn't need more enemies.

There is another sharp edge here. Because the rewards for fraud can be so large, people sometimes cross the line of ethical and honest behavior, and we have another headline deploring either Wall Street or capitalism. The accounting machinations at Enron, Worldcom, and Tyco a few years back and the more recent notoriety

---

76   *Choosing the Road to Prosperity: Why We Must End Too Big To Fail—Now*, 2011 Annual Report, The Federal Reserve Bank of Dallas.

77   Cassidy. "What Good is Wall Street," (2010).

of Bernie Madoff leap to mind. The opportunity for such dishonesty is part of the price of freedom, but because it is blamed on the capitalist system and not just the nature of man, it contributes to the bias against business.

Greed

People decry greed because they don't like the idea that each of us has at least a little bit in our own character.

Self-interest is why the free-market creates wealth and the commune does not. One labors in the free market because it is the path to satisfying one's own needs and wants. In general, more effort produces more reward.

In a commune, one works for the greater good of all. Communes usually last until too many people discover that their share of the common good is substantially less than their input to its production. This is the dominant reason for socialism's failure: it disconnects effort and reward. Effort is not serving one's self-interest, so the motivation for effort dies.

Greed is just very muscular self-interest that only occurs in other people. Self-interest is the motive power that makes a market economy function, but when we call it greed, it takes on a different psychological character. In many minds capitalism is associated with greed rather than self-interest. Greed is actually bad only when it slides into dishonest or unethical behavior.

Recessions

The invisible hand sometimes appears to be attached to a broken wrist. We have been repeatedly afflicted by business cycles and recessions and depressions that have been very painful. There is always highly politicized argument about why they happen; suffice it to say that in modern times they usually involve both the private sector's invisible hand and the government's large finger.

This is a large blemish on the face of economic evolution, and such lapses in good economic performance have been tragic for many people. Unfortunately, there will probably be more in our future.

The Mistrust of Business

Imagine a polling firm asking folks which group they would be most likely to trust based on their answers to the question: *What is your objective?*

The Government says: *To serve the public.*

The Labor Union says: *To serve the worker.*

The Businessman says: *To make a profit.*

(This is a no-brainer.)

The newly hired Public Relations man says to his new client:

"Mr. Businessman, if I were to ask you your objective in dieting, you wouldn't answer 'to use the scales.' Using the scales is just the way you measure progress (or lack thereof) toward your goal. Similarly, the objective of business is at heart

To efficiently satisfy the wants of people.

If your business fails to do that there won't be any profits. Profit is just the measure of your success; it tells you how well you are succeeding. If you don't make a profit you are obviously not satisfying a sufficient number of people. Profit is your discipline, without it you can't stay in the business of satisfying wants."

There is no comparable measure for the efficacy of either government or of the unions. It might be argued that affirmation of the government's performance in serving the public is its political leaders ability to get reelected. Or perhaps the tone of internet chatter can give a clue. Unions measure success by how much they can get for their workers. That is a far too simplistic a measure; it ignores that more for the worker means higher prices for the consumer, a higher cost of capital for the company, and a decreased ability of the company to compete.

Many people do not appreciate how hard it is to succeed in business, to actually make that profit that is necessary if a company is to survive. Approximately one in ten U.S. companies disappear each year. Between 1989 and 1997, an average of 611,000 businesses a year vanished out of a total of 5.73 million firms. Ten percent is the average extinction rate.[78]

Creative-destruction is a tough environment. And business badly needs an improvement in its public relations.

Economic Growth is An Evolutionary Process

Many of the negative perceptions recounted here stem from the fact that few people really understand how our innovative economy works.

The growth in wealth just seems to happen; nobody associates the improvement with the almost continuous stream of innovation taking place in factories, in logistic systems, in all parts of our economy. This innovation is the driver of our increasing wealth, but people don't see the process unfolding. They don't see that it is the capitalist economic system that both motivates and enables this innovation that is producing our rising wealth.

Almost daily headlines remind us of the downsides of capitalism as they happen, as obsolete factories close, or as some CEO declares a $30 million dollar capital gain from the exercise of his stock options. So capitalism's bounty is taken for granted and accepted without attribution, while its warts become constant companions to our consciousness.

There is a danger in having a population that does not understand how the economic system works. People want to dull the sharp edges. In response to their pressure, laws are passed and regulations imposed that are intended to fix this or prevent that.

---

78   Ferguson, The Ascent of Money: A Financial History of the World, (2008), 351.

This is all done under the implicit assumption that the system will nevertheless continue to work its magic because it always has; the goose has always laid golden eggs, surely it won't quit now. They are probably right: it won't quit, but the eggs will get smaller and smaller.

Let us remember that capitalism is not in competition with Heaven, only with all the other economic systems known to man.

CHAPTER 4 - THE ROLE AND IMPACT OF GOVERNMENT

The government is and will continue to be the central actor in the nation's ongoing evolution. This chapter aims to provide a perspective on the functions of government that have the greatest influence on the performance of the economy. Subsequent chapters will address the primary problems that have manifested themselves over the years and possible directions for their alleviation. The focus continues on this nation, the United States.

Taxing and Spending

With a few very small exceptions, *the private sector produces all the goods and services produced by the economy*. The money—the Gross Domestic Product (GDP)—that represents these outputs is used in three different ways.

The government gets paid first, so the first area of disbursement by the private sector is in the payment of taxes. Much of that money is put back into the private sector as the government purchases goods and services and provides direct payments to people.

Of what is left after taxes are paid, people use one part to support their daily lives—their food and housing, their playthings, and so on. This is consumption; it funds the way people live.

The other part is saved. That doesn't mean it goes under the mattress, although that can happen. It usually deposited in a bank or used to buy stocks or bonds. These savings are the source of money used by entrepreneurs and business people to do new things—start a new business or expand an old one, buy a new machine or improve an old one, or pursue an invention. This saved money is the source of the investment needed to fuel innovation and keep the economy healthy and growing.[79]

So if the taxes are extracted from the monies that would have otherwise been used in consumption, those taxes tend to reduce living standards. Those taken from potential investment funds penalize the potential growth prospects for the economy. Whether the taxes come from investment or consumption depends on the technique of extraction.

At the federal level the primary methods of extraction are the taxes on income, including that on capital gains; the tax on corporate profits; and tax to support Social Security, the FICA tax[80]. There are others, but these are the relevant ones here.

Sales taxes and property taxes are the largest taxes at the state and local levels. The myriad of other taxes and fees can't help but make one proud to be part of a society that has leaders with so much ingenuity and imagination.

Summarizing, essentially all wealth, measured by the GDP, is generated by the private sector, and is expended in three ways. Consumption expenditures buy goods and services to provide for our immediate living. What is not consumed is saved, and is potentially invested, producing growth in the economy. The government extracts taxes for its use from both consumption and investment.

Forms of Taxation: Income Taxes

In 2008 the top 50 percent of people in the U. S. who filed an income tax report received 87 percent of the income and paid 97

---

79   We don't want to get hung up on National Income Accounting terminology. For example, from the point of view of the individual, buying stock in a company is an investment, but under NIA it only becomes an investment when the business actually spends money .
80   Federal Insurance Contribution Act

percent of the taxes. The bottom 50 percent made 13 percent of the income and paid 3 percent of the taxes. The top 1 percent of filers made 20 percent of the income and paid 38 percent of the income taxes.[81]

Like beauty, *fair* is a very illusive concept, here to be ignored in preference to economic considerations.

Since lower income people typically use all of their income to live, nearly all direct investment is made by people with higher incomes. The qualifier "direct" is made because anyone with a pension plan is an investor—the plan's custodian invests for them.

The fact that investment primarily comes from high-income folks immediately leads some to the conclusion that the best taxes to promote growth would be regressive; that is, tilted so the lower incomes pay the most tax.

It is true that taxes drawn from consumption rather than potential investment allows greater growth, but the judgment that regressive taxes are therefore preferable may be too quick. Most affluent individuals get a high percentage of their income from investments, so may be reluctant to reduce that income; they may well chose to maintain their level of investment and pay their taxes from what they would have spent on consumption—on their standard of living. I have not seen any data on this issue.

It is hard to argue that a person who makes $20 million a year can't give up $2 million without suffering too much or having his investment program severely penalized. How about $4 million; does this level cut into investment? Does serious loss start at $6 million, or $8 million? At what point do people decide they are so heavily taxed that they move to where they are not? Might they decide to leave the country for someplace more tax-friendly?[82]

---

81   Internal Revenue Service, "Individual Income Tax Returns with Positive Adjusted Gross Income (AGI) Returns Classified by Tax Percentile - Early Release"

82   Economics Professor Richard Vedder found a distinct tax-induced migration from the 10 highest tax states to the 10 lowest tax states during the period studied (4-1-2000 through 6-30-2004). Taxes Fuel Historic American Migration. *The Heartland Institute*, (12-1-2005)

The fact is that we do not know at what level these things might start to happen. There may be some tipping point, or maybe it is just a gradual phenomenon.

Why should we care? We should care because these are the people who are not only the dominant source of funds for new investments, but they are also many of the entrepreneurs with the personal attributes to drive the innovative process. So a serious consideration in imposing high taxes on the wealthy is how much these geese can be plucked before the eggs are in danger.

Forms of Taxation: Capital Gains

Taxes on capital gains tend to reduce investment because this tax lowers the expected return on investment without lowering the risk. Thus the capital gains tax rate is a very important factor in determining whether an investment will be made at all.

This point is illustrated by a story, possibly apocryphal but accurate in its implications, about the surprisingly large number of Rolls-Royce automobiles in England in the early '50s. The country had largely turned socialist after WWII, the economy was sinking, and there was a dire need for investment to revive it. So how could people buy all those expensive cars when the country was so poor and needed investment so badly? The answer given was that when anybody with capital to invest thought about the high capital gain taxes they would have to pay on any possible returns, their reaction was, "Screw it, I'll buy a Rolls." High capital gains tax rates pushed money out of investment into consumption.

Forms of Taxation: Social Security

Social Security is described by the government as a system where contributions (the FICA tax) are collected from folks' income. These funds pay current retiree benefits and any excess is invested in government bonds in a trust fund. That fund is used to make up the difference when FICA collections fall short.

That description leaves out one little detail. The FICA funds are collected and are used to pay current benefits just as described. In past years the funds collected have been larger than the funds paid out to retirees, but instead of the excess being put in trust, it was spent exactly the same as other taxes. The trust fund got an IOU from the Congress. Now the payout is larger than the FICA collections. Since the so-called trust fund is full of IOUs[83] instead of money, the Congress pays current beneficiaries the only way it can—with ordinary tax revenues.

Strip away all this bookkeeping, and the net effect is the same as if all FICA were dumped in general revenues, and all benefits paid from general revenues. FICA taxes are spent exactly the same way as all other taxes: none are invested, or spent differently than other kind of tax. Social Security benefits are actually paid from currently collected taxes, disguised by some sleight-of-hand accounting.

Forms of Taxation: Taxes on Business

Another kind of tax is on the profits of private sector businesses. Any tax on corporations tilts heavily toward being a tax on investment, because it would otherwise be available to the company to invest for its own purposes.

The money that corporations use to pay taxes came from the people who bought their products, which have to be priced higher to cover the extra expense of the tax. Actually, it's not clear who pays the corporate tax: the extra cost it imposes on the corporation may be partly covered by slightly lower wages, slightly higher prices, slightly lower dividends for the stockholders, and slightly less profit for reinvestment (which tends to lower the price of the stock). Thus

---

83    $2.6 trillions worth according to the May 13, 2011 report from the Social Security Administration's Board of Trustees.

the corporate tax is indirectly another tax on individuals collected through what appears to be an unnecessarily complex path.

Forms of Taxation: Sales and VAT (value added tax)

A pure sales tax is mostly a tax on consumption because more sales are made to support consumption than sales in support of investment. If food is excluded from the tax, it becomes more of a mixed bag.

A version of the sales tax is the value added tax, or VAT. This is tax imposed during the production of products so it gets built into the retail price. Like the sales tax, it is largely on consumption. There are many who fear it because it is hidden enough that it is the easiest tax for legislatures to jack up without causing much political objection. On the other hand, it is less likely to be evaded by barter transactions—in which no money changes hands— than the sales tax. The VAT is widely used in Europe.

Where Taxes Go—Government Spending

In FY2011 the gross domestic product (GDP)—all goods and services produced in the country—was $15.3 trillion. This was augmented by another $0.6 trillion of imported goods and services. Of this total, 68 percent was consumed, 13 percent was invested, and 19 percent spent by federal, state, and local governments.[84]

The governments actually collected over 25 percent of our GDP in taxes, and borrowed another 8 percent, but passed much of it back to the people in transfer payments, mostly in Social Security benefits.[85] I conjecture that most Social Security ends up in consumption. Since the taxes came predominantly from those folks most likely to be investors, the net effect is to convert some potential investment into consumption.

---

84 Bureau of Economic Ayanysis, Table 1.1.5. Gross National Product
85 Bureau of Economic Ayanysis, Table 3.1. Government Current Reciepts and Expenditures

The federal government spent roughly 21 percent for Medicare, Medicaid, and the Children's Health Insurance Program); 20 percent for defense and security, 20 percent for Social Security; 13 percent for other safety net programs; 7 percent on federal and veteran retirees; 6 percent for interest on the debt; 3 percent on transportation and infrastructure; 3 percent on education; 2 percent on scientific and medical research; 1 percent on non-security foreign aid; and 4 percent on everything else.[86]

Because the government does spend some of the taxes collected on things that improve private sector productivity—like build roads, enforce the law, do R&D (research and development) in many areas— some of this money collected as taxes is almost functionally equivalent to private sector investment. Depending on what one counts, maybe 5 to 10 percent of the federal budget could be included in this category.

Government Spending: Subsidies

The government often decides that some business or endeavor has value beyond that which is accorded to it by normal economic evaluation in the market place. For example, a large company that raised corn persuaded the Congress that we could save oil by burning corn-derived fuel in our vehicles. Since nobody would buy ethanol at its true cost, the Congress decided to divert some taxes to pay part of its cost. So we subsidized the ethanol that was mixed in our gasoline. The side effect was that the corn we eat was made more expensive. In order to protect the domestic ethanol program, the government instituted protective tariffs to discourage the use of cheaper ethanol made in Brazil from sugarcane.

The federal government subsidizes farming, windmills and other nonfossil energy sources, electric cars (which use electricity partially generated by burning coal), housing, and so on. The *Catalog of Federal Domestic Assistance* provides an official listing

---

86   Policy Basics:"Where Do Our Federal Tax Dollars Go?," Center on Budget and Policy Priorities.

of all federal aid (or subsidy) programs, including grants, loans, insurance, scholarships, and other types of cash and noncash benefits. In 2006 it was 2437 pages long and listed 1696 programs, up from 1425 in 2005.[87]

It is improbable that many of these programs would have been provided by the private sector; whether they are worth their cost lies in the eyes of some very influential beholder.

In addition to taxing and spending, the third area of government's influence on the economic performance of the private sector is regulation, the next subject of discussion.

Why Regulation?

There are two areas of regulation that are generally accepted as necessary, and even here there is wide disagreement as to the right degree. The first is to preserve the safety, health, and environmental standards of society.

It costs money to do things like equip machinery so that it is less likely to cut off fingers, prevent rats from adding unwanted ingredients to the grain, or to cleanly dispose of that nasty effluent instead of dumping it into the river. If manufacturer A pays the price to be Mr. Clean, then Manufacturer B, who is less civic minded, can undersell him and put Manufacturer A out of business. So the only way to make everybody clean up is to impose a regulation.

The second area of necessary regulation is that needed to preserve competition in commercial activity. Regulation is needed because the self-interest of most participants is better served by avoiding competition.

John, the baker, doesn't bake his bread because he likes to give bread to his fellow man; he bakes and sells bread because it is a way to put food on his own table.

Now on the face of it, it is in John's self-interest to charge as much as his customers will allow, which may be well above the price

---

87   Cato Institute Tax and Budget Bulletin, No. 41, Oct. 2006.

necessary for him to stay in business. The reason he does not is because Sam, the baker down the street, would then undersell him. But if John and Sam can agree on a high price for bread, they can both take in much more money than their cost. So the temptation is to collude to avoid competing. Thus the need for regulation to prevent such anticompetitive behavior.

If competition is maintained, both Sam and John are encouraged to find better ways to bake bread, because it serves their own self-interest to do so. So self-interest combined with competition is the real regulator of prices and quality, and fosters both innovation and the efficient use of resources.

There are many dimensions to competition. There is regulation to try to insure truth in advertising. The anti-trust laws are intended to militate against companies buying or combining with other companies to gain some monopolistic advantage. There is *playing field competition*: corporations and labor unions use the influence they gained by contributing to election campaigns to have the regulatory or tax codes or trade rules tweaked to favor their own interests at the expense of their rivals. It is very hard to regulate against this crony-capitalism.

Last, there is competition that is regulated not by the government, but by the market. Professor Schumpeter had the following to say about this kind of competition:

"But in capitalist reality...it is not (the textbook) kind of competition that counts but the competition from the new commodity, the new technology, the new source of supply, the new type of organization — competition which commands a decisive cost or quality advantage and which strikes not at the margins of the profits and the outputs of the existing firms but at their foundations and their very lives."[88]

This, of course, is the competition of innovation.

A more controversial area of regulation is the financial sector of the economy. The primary purposes of financial regulation are, first, to protect savers and investors from bank failures

88   Schumpeter, *Capitalism, Socialism and Democracy*, (1942), 84.

and various forms of cheating, and, second, to insure financial stability of the system in the face of the various and many shocks that it can encounter from both man and nature. The latter is a challenge that has yet to be met satisfactorily; the answer may or may not be found in extensive regulation; there are many who argue that provisions that appear to protect against failure drive out prudence, and therefore encourage bankers to increase risk. The issue remains open, very open.

Last, there are kinds of regulations dealing with licenses to do certain jobs, codes governing all kinds of construction, medical equipment and drug approval processes, and probably dozens of areas that I have forgotten or know nothing about.

Clearly it is not realistic to say that there is absolutely no need for regulation. We have not yet found a way to organize society so that the incentives people face all lead to desirable behavior.

Creating Regulation: the Seen and the Unseen[89]

The Energy Policy and Conservation Act of 1975 established the so-called CAFÉ (Corporate Average Fuel Economy) standards. These mandated that the average miles per gallon of the fleet of cars sold by car manufacturers could not drop below a certain average-miles-per-gallon number. Now everyone is in favor of good policy and who could possibly be against conservation and better gas mileage. All that was clearly the *seen* part of the Act.

Predictably, the way the automobile manufactures met these new standards was by building smaller cars. Since small cars can't do as good a job of protecting occupants in an accident as larger cars, they have a higher death and injury rate than large cars.

So the *seen* was the gasoline to be saved. The *unseen* was the price to be exacted of more deaths and injuries in the smaller cars.

---

89   Courtesy of Frederic Bastiat, *That Which is Seen and That Which is Unseen.* (1850) http://bastiat.org/en/twisatwins.html

That particular *unseen* is now part of the *seen*, but it has not changed the assessment of the program; there are proposals afoot to further lower the miles per gallon number.[90]

The CAFÉ standards were introduced because rising oil prices frightened people into thinking the world was running out of oil. The biggest *unseen* was the scenario that might have happened if the government had done nothing. It is reasonable to assume that higher gas prices would have made cars with the better gas mileage more competitive in the marketplace. It is also reasonable to assume that automobile manufacturers would have therefore put more effort into producing cars with better mileage. The consequences of the do-nothing option remain *unseen*.

Ideally, regulations would only be put in place after foresight and analysis had changed all the *unseens* into *seens*, after costs of all kinds had been identified, estimated, and weighed against their anticipated benefits. In the real world, full of uncertainty and emotion, it's a rare case that either benefits or costs can be completely agreed on by everybody.

The Bias is Toward Too Much Regulation

When there is a call to "do something," most legislators want to do something; it is in their self-interest to satisfy their voters and be as helpful as they think they can to the benefactors of their reelection funds. So here, too, the incentives bias toward action rather than restraint. Too often the result is badly aimed overreaction.

When the rash of accounting scandals (Enron, Worldcom, Tyco) occurred in 2000 to 2002 there was great pressure "do something." The Congress did something; it passed the Sarbanes-Oxley Act

---

90   The causes of traffic fatalities are complex, and there is considerable uncertainty in the size of the smaller car penalty. Apparently it has been considered small enough that the trade-off favors making the CAFÉ standards more stringent. See the study by the National Research Council's Board on Energy and Environmental Systems, 2002.

which introduced many new standards and increased oversight of the accounting in public companies.[91]

The wide disagreement now over the net desirability of Sarbanes-Oxley is inconsistent with its overwhelming approval in the immediate aftermath of the scandals. The vote in the House was 423 to 3 with 8 abstentions, 99 in the Senate with 1 abstention. Would the approval have been so marked if the bill had been delayed to permit a longer period for cooling off and thoughtful analysis? Would it have been made less stringent, which is the primary objection to it now? A few weeks or months delay before taking action on a change that was to have a substantial impact for years to come would not have been an exorbitant price, but the incentive facing the legislators was to act, not to wait.

The implication of this example is that the incentive to satisfy an impatient public leads legislators and bureaucracies to act too precipitously to allow careful consideration of the issue involved. It is highly probable that the passage of the Dodd-Frank Wall Street Reform and Consumer Protection Act in 2010 is a replay-writ-large of the Sarbanes-Oxley overreaction.

When the crisis du jour strikes the best thing to do is often nothing; the problem will succumb to the spontaneous actions taken by the many actors in the context of the free market *as if guided by an invisible hand*. But it is very hard for a politician to do nothing when loud voices are crying, "Do something; the sky is falling." So the President or the Congress often does something, without a pause for cooling off and thinking, and that something is almost always a new set of regulations, full of *unseens*.

The bias extends to the bureaucracy, the people who translate the laws into specific *Thou shalts* and *Thou shalt nots*. For them, the *seen* is failure to prevent whatever was intended to be prevented. The cost of going too far is the *unseen*, or at least it is still the preferred direction for error.

---

91   Public Company Accounting Reform and Investor Protection Act of 2002.

Regulation has grown impressively. The Code of Federal Regulations (CFR), the official listing of all federal-level regulations in effect, contained nearly fifty-five thousand pages in 1970. In 1998 it had grown to almost one hundred and thirty-five thousand pages, and by 2007 it was close to tripling to one hundred and forty-six thousand pages. In 2008 these volumes took up over twenty-five feet of shelf space in the Library of Congress.[92] Hammurabi would be very impressed.

The Quest for the Risk-Free Society

People have too much faith that regulations can take the risks out of life. Anytime something goes wrong the choice is either to accept that a metaphorical sheep does get lost now and then, or, in our quest for a risk-free society, figuratively hire another shepherd.

There is a serious danger in this bias. Shepherds seldom go away, they just accumulate. Every shepherd, every regulation, constrains in some way the decisions made by people. A regulation says you cannot do A or B or C. Or it may say you must do X. The regulation has already made part of the decision of what to do, or what not to do.

The net effect is therefore to take more decisions out of the private sector's invisible hand and move them to the state, pre-made. So regulation moves the economic system toward the socialist model; it puts a splint on the invisible hand. We know we need some regulation for various reasons; the difficulty is knowing when to stop.

Foreign Trade

Another area in which the government seriously impacts the behavior of the private sector is in foreign trade. In Chapter 1 it was described how widening markets increased the opportunity

---

92   Hayes, *Are Federal Regulations Too Numerous? Has The Number of Them Multiplied Excessively?*

for specialization, innovation, and increases in scale—with all their economic benefits. Foreign trade does this even more effectively than widening domestic markets because it is much more likely to bring new thinking and novel methods and products into view. Free trade, minimally encumbered by governments, is much to be desired for the world.

In theory, when the U.S. trades with another nation it is just like Arizona trading with Illinois, except for a few complications. First, the currencies are different between countries, so some agreement has to be reached as to the conversion ratio.[93] Second, the rules of the economic game differ between countries. The economic principles are the same, but the rules they play by are different. These differences can lead to huge complexities.

Many people are convinced that the object of trade is for us to sell more to foreign nations than they do to us, believing the bigger the imbalance the better it is for us. The economist Frank Knight observed: *"The man from Mars reading the typical pronouncements of our best financial writers or statesmen could hardly avoid the conclusion that a nation's prosperity depends upon getting rid of the greatest possible amount of goods and avoiding the receipt of anything tangible in payment for them."*[94]

There are consequences from imbalances. If we buy more from foreign nations than they do from us, then we owe them the difference in value between our and their imports. They may just lend this difference back to us by buying our bonds, since a bond is just an IOU on which we would pay them interest. Or they may spend the difference on things that aren't exports so they don't count in the trade balance, like a factory in Georgia or stock from the New York Stock Exchange.

---

93   The perspective of viewing foreign trade as analogous to interstate trade was used by Murray N. Rothbard in his monograph "Protectionism and the Destruction of Property", *Mises Institute* (1986).

94   Frank H. Knight, "Historical and Theoretical Issues in the Problem of Modern Capitalism," *Journal of Economics and Business History*, Nov. 1928; reprinted in F.H. Knight, *On the History and Method of Economics* (1956), pp. 89-103; the quotation from page 91.

Obviously, a large imbalance that went on forever would lead to running out of the ability to borrow, or to some foreign country owning all our assets. But the U.S. is a very big nation, so it would have to be a extremely large imbalance that went on for a long time to matter very much. But such imbalances do not go on forever; they are brought toward balance by shifts in exchange rates, and relative changes in the internal economies of the nations involved.

Sometimes imbalances are caused by changes in relative competitiveness in particular industries.[95] There are generally two reactions to inability to compete. The first is to have domestic companies or their unions argue that the foreigners are cheating somehow: they are getting subsidy from their government, they are using child labor, or they are damaging the environment. The second step is to therefore plead that the domestic industry needs the protection of high tariffs on the competing products to make competition "fair". If the tariffs are granted, the *seen* result is that the complaining company or industry can continue in its less competitive ways; the *unseen* result is that the general populace continues to pay higher prices than necessary for the products affected.

Here is a quote from a Cato Institute study:[96] *"The most principled case (for free trade) is a moral one: voluntary economic exchange is inherently fair, benefits both parties, and allocates scarce resources more efficiently than a system under which government dictates or limits choices. Moreover, government intervention in voluntary economic exchange on behalf of some citizens necessarily comes at the expense of others and is inherently unfair, inefficient, and subverts the rule of law. At their core, trade barriers are the triumph of coercion and politics over free choice and economics. Trade barriers are the result of productive resources being diverted to achieve political ends*

---

95   Our big three automakers and their unions have had considerable experience with this kind of situation.

96   "Beyond Exports: A Better Case for Free Trade", Daniel J. Ikenson & Scott Lincicome, *Cato Institute, Free Trade Bulletin* no. 43

and, in the process, taxing unsuspecting consumers to line the pockets of the special interests that succeeded in enlisting the weight of the government on their side."

The world would be better off if trade were completely free, but that seems only a distant hope.

Uncertainty Discourages Investment

There is one more way that the behavior of government affects the investment behavior of the private sector: by changing or threatening to change the rules of the game.

There is seldom a lack of ideas for a new investment. For potential investors the issue is deciding if the return on their possible investment is likely to be good enough to justify the risk. This involves projecting into the future one's best idea of how events might unfold, and estimating the monetary return that might be reasonably expected. To do that one has to make assumptions as to what the taxes will be on these returns, and how regulatory and foreign trade rules that might also affect the return and the risk. These factors are a key part the evaluation of any potential investment.

These tax and regulatory policies define the rules of the game. If there is serious concern that those policies might be changed in the future, then all calculations of return on investment within those defined and understood rules are thrown into doubt, adding one more element of risk.

The situation is starker if the potential investor absolutely knows that they will be changed, but not how the changes will affect him. This happens if major legislation is passed mandating new regulations, but the actual regulations have yet to be formulated, a process that might take several years. This situation provides a strong incentive to do nothing until the new rules are defined. This was the case in 2010 and 2011 when the new healthcare and the Dodd-Frank bills had been passed, portending substantial regulatory change in coming years that could only be guessed at.

The Quest for Balance

There is no question that government policies, regulations, taxes, trade rules, and consistency of policy have become a foremost part of the calculus of private sector behavior. There is almost no aspect of life not directly touched by government.

The incentive structure within government produces a bias toward too much interference with the free market. The incentive perceived by the elected public servant is to satisfy the electorate looking for both largess and a freedom from risk and unpleasantness, and to satisfy the need for campaign funding by catering to potential benefactors who are looking for competitive advantage in their own endeavors. For the bureaucracy responsible for interpreting a particular law into specific regulations, the incentive is to both avoid criticism and to increase influence.

The *completely unconstrained free-market* is precluded by the frailties of people; we are not angels. The ideal would be a *rationally constrained market*—if we could only agree on what is rational; what constitutes such a market lies to a high degree in the eyes of the beholder. The bias that exists is strongly toward overregulation—toward too many shepherds. Many fear that this bias is sliding us into a *government-smothered market*, and down the road toward a very low growth, state-run society.

CHAPTER 5 - THE HAZARDS OF DEMOCRACY

We the People...

So begins the Constitution of the United States. These three words launched our nation on the boldest experiment in governance the world had ever known: giving the people the responsibility to chose their rulers. We have now lived this experiment for well over two hundred years; if we can last another five hundred we will have tied the Romans in longevity.

By and large, it has been a successful experiment. But far from perfect: one has to ask just why the government is afraid to restructure our runaway entitlement programs so they are affordable, why we spend so much money we don't have, why the government goes too far in regulating business, why the tax code is so ridiculously complex and progressive, why it institutes "protective" tariffs to the detriment of consumers, why it has taken on responsibilities that would have been better left to the private sector.

I do not believe that the answer is because most of the political leaders we elect are incompetent. A large part of the answer lies in the structure of democratic government itself and the incentives that structure puts in place.

The Imbalance in Political Power

Most people dislike having to think about an unfamiliar scenario that is inconsistent with their familiar beliefs. Here you are asked to do just that.

Our nation is a democratic republic. Thus the country is actually governed by leaders who are elected by the voters. These leaders are acutely aware that their jobs depend on pleasing the voters. They compete for these jobs by presenting to the voters their various visions of how the government should work and what they would do if elected.

It takes a politician who is brave to the point of foolish to fly very far in the face of the preferences of his or her constituents. Political aspirants can and should try to shape their constituent's minds on issues, but can't afford to push to the point of losing their support. So in order to be elected, our politician is biased toward molding his message, his promises, to appeal to his constituents, the voters. If his actual behavior in office deviates too markedly from these promises, he jeopardizes his reelection.

So by their choice of leaders the voters really do determine the primary policies, and sometimes particular specifics, that the nation is to embrace.

Who, then, are these voters who select our leaders and thereby determine how the nation is to be run?

When the Constitution was adopted, it said nothing about who could vote; that was left to the states. At that time the vote was largely restricted to adult white male property owners. Thus the power to have a say in the choice of leaders—the political power—was allocated to only those citizens whose property ownership gave them a direct economic stake in the country, who had "skin in the game."

By 1840 federal legislation had broadened voting rights to all white males and dropped the property requirement. By legislation and Constitutional amendment the vote has been successively broadened to now include most adult citizens.

This progressive broadening of the franchise was at least partially motivated by a sense of fairness; it was felt that people who were part of the fabric of the nation should have some say in how the nation was run. I conjecture that the decision to broaden the franchise did not omit consideration of where the new voters were likely to direct their political support.

So now every adult citizen has the vote. What can we say about this state of affairs?

In 2008 almost 94 percent of the employed people between 25 and 64 years old had incomes under $100,000 a year, and about 70 percent had incomes under $50,000. Only slightly over 6 percent had incomes over $100,000.[97] The obvious point is that lower-income voters outnumber middle- and high-income voters by a huge margin.

Higher-income neighborhoods, on average, have better public schools than low-income neighborhoods. Higher-income parents can afford more private schooling than can lower-income parents. Higher-income folks invest more, and have greater motivation to keep abreast of economic conditions. Higher-income folks pay higher taxes; slightly more than half of earners pay no federal income tax at all. These factors are high among the considerations that lead to the following assertion:

Acceding to many individual exceptions, higher income folks have a higher probability of having had better educational opportunities, a better understanding of public finance and economics, have more invested in the economy, pay more taxes, and are more motivated to stay aware of governmental behavior than lower income folks.

Since there are far more people in the lower income group, the end of the spectrum least prepared and motivated to vote carefully and with discrimination, and who contribute the least monetarily to the economy, is accorded by far the greatest political power.

---

97   *"Personal Income in the United States,"* Wikipedia. Data from the Census Bureau.

Incentives mold behavior, and self-interest is the most common yardstick by which people evaluate alternatives. Self-interest leads most people to vote their pocketbook. The implication is obvious: the politician who promises to fatten those pocketbooks gains a political advantage and is therefore tempted to make such promises. *Fiscal prudence is a political disadvantage.*

Anyone who is paying attention has known for years that our entitlement programs are not affordable as they stand, and should be restructured. Most beneficiaries of these programs fear that any relief to the program's very serious fiscal problems will result in lessening the largess they provide, so the politician who proposes to change them is risking his job. The result is that the problem has festered because of the political fear to touch it.

The nation needs a safety net for the unfortunate. Lower-income voters general favor a wide net with a fine mesh. Such a net is more expensive, so the bias is toward greater spending.

Our highly progressive income tax is a symptom of this political power imbalance. In the 20 years since 1987 the federal income taxes paid by the top 20 percent of households has increased from 57 percent to 70 percent. By 2009 51 percent of earners paid no income tax at all.[98]

Having little or no skin in the game reduces the incentive for lower income voters to pay attention to the government's general behavior, and, in particular, its use of taxes and its general fiscal posture.

So the fact that the dominant political power is given to the less-rich voters results in a failure of the government to restructure unsustainable entitlements, a general propensity to spend too easily, and an income tax structure that is more likely to tax investment than consumption.

It is hard not to believe that this imbalance in political power has been a major factor in bringing our national debt and unfunded

---

98   John D.McKinnon, "High-Earning Households Pay Growing Share of Taxes," *Wall Street Journal*, May 3, 2011.

future promises to dangerous levels. The public debt of the U.S. is now roughly equal to our GDP (100 percent of GDP), and the unfunded liabilities built into our entitlement programs are huge. The fact that the nation can still borrow more (sell bonds) at very low interest rates only signals that lenders are not yet concerned that we could fail to pay these debts or cope with our liabilities.

It is sobering, though, to look at other countries. The Greeks are deepest in the hole. Greek voters have fairly consistently supported the Socialist Party, furthering a welfare state and a large bureaucracy. High tax rates have driven a fourth of the economy underground. The big problem, though, is public pressure that makes it very hard to stop spending. In 2010 their debt was 165 percent of their GDP,[99] and their prospects for restraining it are poor. Their ability to continue to borrow appears to have run out. This drama is still playing; other countries in a similar plight are waiting in the wings.

Can We Do Better?

An interesting idea for a more balanced voting system was described by Nevil Shute in his novel *In The Wet*, published over fifty years ago. He hypothesized a voting system for an Australia thirty years in his future. Every adult had one vote. If one had a college degree they got a second vote. Certain public service jobs earned a third vote. And so on to where, as I recall, the head of their Supreme Court could have earned a total of seven votes. This was obviously aimed at awarding political power more closely in proportion to the individual's contribution to the society.

The Romans had a different approach to keeping political power roughly aligned with contributions to the financing of the nation. All their voting was done in two stages. Voters were assigned to groups on the basis of their wealth, which was also the basis for the taxes levied on them. Each group held their own vote on the issue or election at hand. Then each group had an assigned number of votes

---

99   The Greek Crisis, *The Christian Science Monitor*, Dec. 3, 2011

to be rendered as a block in the deciding tally. The first group, the patricians—the old families and most of the political leadership—had eighteen votes to use as one block. The next group, the very wealthy, had eighty votes. There were then groups of progressively less wealthy men, the top three groups having twenty votes each, the last and much larger group having thirty votes. The very poorest, and probably the largest group, had only 1 vote (ostensibly because they didn't pay any taxes). Note that the patricians and the very rich together had 98 votes, more than half the total.[100]

Such a heavy tilt to the very wealthy is not appropriate for a free people where everyone should have some voice. But the tilt should give a stronger voice to the people who actually pay the bills; this is appropriate not primarily because it fits most people's notion of fairness, but because this should at least partially alleviate the current bias toward fiscal imprudence.

The illustrative allocation offered here is aimed at giving the most political power to the middle class. Everyone gets one vote, as they do now. Then everyone who paid some nominal amount of income tax would get a second vote. The amount selected should be such that eighty or ninety percent of all income taxpayers gets a second vote. The third vote should be more expensive, say, twice this base amount. The fourth should be still more expensive, maybe four times the base level. And so on. This would allocate the most political power to those who pay taxes, but gives the most influence to the middle class. The votes allocated to the rich and the very rich are tempered by the increasing 'price' for additional votes. In these days of computers, it would be fairly straightforward to implement such a system.

This should help take some of the sting out of paying taxes, and make it politically easier to widen the tax base because the promise of a second vote would add a bit of sugar coating to having to pay

---

100 Durant, *Caesar and Christ*, (1944), 26. Some issues were determined by a second method of voting, based on residence. It was dominated by land-owning farmers, very conservative men.

taxes. It wouldn't be surprising if having extra votes began to be a point of pride.

While not the primary motivation for expanding the franchise as described, it is very hard to defend the current system on the basis of fairness, with the people paying most of the nation's bills having the least say in how the nations is run. Most people agree with the general principle that whoever pays the fiddler should call the tune.

The text for a bumper sticker has already been successfully tested:

No taxation without representation.

Now this system of giving out *tax compensation votes* may be a wonderful idea when another continent is discovered somewhere and a new nation is to be formed, but here and now there is little possibility that such a scheme could be given much consideration. It flies in the face of the notion that we all deserve to be equal, and it would be asking the people with the most political power to vote away some of that power.

But stranger things have happened. It took a very long time for men to decide that their exclusive political power should be diluted by letting women vote. Change happens.

Incentives Matter

Many folks see themselves as just pawns in society. Because they have no skin in the game, they have little incentive to care much about how the nation is run. They see government giving out money for all kinds of things, and happily support politicians who promise to get some of it for them. *The need here is to shift people's primary interest from the golden eggs to the health of the goose that's laying them.*

It would be a big step in the right direction if it became very plain to everyone that his or her retirement income depended directly on the long-term health of the economy. One obvious way to do that is to modify the Social Security system.

Social Security is now a *defined benefit* system—a system under which the amount of the benefit to be paid to retirees is predetermined and ostensibly guaranteed. The size of these payments is calculated using a formula based on the contributions made throughout one's working life, but tilted by internal cross-subsidies to give the lower-income contributors a better shake.[101] The benefits are paid from taxes collected at the time of payout.

Most people see nothing wrong with that; they see no reason to fret about getting paid because the government has always paid before and the government obviously has plenty of money. They do not recognize that the ability of the government to make those payments also depends on the long-term health of the economy: if the economy fails to grow, then the tax revenue available for payout will be inadequate, forcing at some point painful cuts in benefits.[102]

With a *defined contribution* pension, the size of one's contribution is specified just as with a defined benefit system, but the benefits depend entirely on how much the invested contributions have grown by the time of retirement. Individual retirement accounts (IRAs) and 401(k)s are defined benefit plans whose payout depends on the growth in specific investments. For a defined contribution Social Security the investments are envisioned to be spread over the whole economy, thus making everyone's retirement income directly dependent on the nation's long-term growth, not on guessing right on the fate of particular stocks or bonds.

Under a defined contribution Social Security system everyone becomes an investor, and interest in economic matters should spread from the board room and the cocktail party to the barbeque, the ball field, and the bar. With everyone interested in how his or

---

101 Francine J. Lipman, and James E. Williamson, Social Security Benefits Formula 101 (April 29, 2011). *Orange County Lawyer*, May 2011.

102 This is a reality that may be very close to being brought home.

her Social Security at retirement is shaping up, the state of the economy will always be front-page news. There will be almost continuous commentary aimed at the general public about how the government's latest action is likely to affect everyone's retirement. With everyone having lots of skin in the game, interest in how the game is being played should increase substantially.

Investing in the broad health of the economy is equivalent to investing in the total stock market. This is scary; people are acutely aware of the market's sometimes treacherous behavior, and this has always been the biggest deterrent to making all or part of Social Security directly dependent on economic growth. The market's record in most decade-long periods has at least one attention-getting down movement, but the long-term trend has always been up, just as has the wealth of the nation. The stock market crash in 1929, with a great deal of 'help' from the government, ushered in a decade of severe depression and a net stock market loss; the twenty seven years from 1942 to 1969 was an almost continuous climb; the 70s were turbulent without net gain; the twenty years from 1980 to 2000 was a period of strong gain—one can barely find the very scary drop in 1987 it was up again so quickly (the government at the time did exactly the right thing: it just ignored it, rather than 'doing something' to 'help'); and the period since 2000 has been another period of scary turbulence with little net change.

The Federal Reserve Bank of St. Louis performed a comparison of private investment versus Social Security, assuming someone had paid into a defined contribution account all his or her working life. The study noted: "*Although a common criticism of investing future retirement funds in the stock market is the risk of a significant downturn in the market at the time of retirement, our analysis considered the recent market downturn and all other downturns over the past 56 years. Despite these market fluctuations, a long-term investment in the S&P 500 for a 2003 retiree would have yielded a greater monthly income than is provided under the current Social Security system.*" [103]

I am tempted to say that downturns as deep and long as the Great Depression in the 1930s are things of the past, but the subprime fiasco happening all around us now is a brutal reminder that the world is too full of surprises to deny that bad things can happen. But a lot has been and is being learned about the behavior of the economy, and a more interested and better-educated populace should be much more vigilant if government again ignores economic realty and tries to do things like the actions that caused this latest recession.

It does seem realistic to suggest that the odds of repeating the mistakes of the past should decrease substantially in the future. Unfortunately there are no guarantees, and public fervor can lead to very bad economic judgment.

But a lengthy recession can significantly impact just a twenty or even thirty-year record, which argues that a switch to private investments shouldn't be made for anyone very close to retirement. This argues for a hybrid system, heavily tilted toward defined benefit for older worker grading to entirely defined contribution for those under about 40 or so.

It makes eminent sense for younger people to opt for private retirement accounts that depend totally on economic growth; they could end up very wealthy at retirement, and on their death their heirs would inherit anything that remained of their possibly very substantial Social Security nest egg.

Social Security based on private accounts has the additional advantage of helping economic growth by increasing the investment funds available to the nation.

Chile introduced a major defined contribution element to its national retirement system in 1980. It retains an element of defined benefit, in that a minimum level of payments is promised. Now

---

103 Garrett and Rhine. "*Social Security versus Private Retirement Accounts: A Historical Analysis.*" (2005), 115.

over thirty years old, it seems to be very successful.[104]Australia also has a retirement system with both a defined benefit and a defined contribution element. The Australian national system was established in 1992; this system also appears to be quite popular.[105]

Now the focus shifts to a different hazard of democracy: crony capitalism.

The Price of Getting Elected

The essential requirement to become a member of Congress or a President is to get elected. From a politician's perspective, only if they get elected (or reelected), can they do all the wonderful things for the nation that motivated their desire for a career in public service. Failing election, nothing else matters much.

Running for election is very expensive. Unless our budding politician is extremely rich, he or she must get campaign money from someplace. The pressure to raise this money is powerful; without money a candidate is not going to become a public servant.

Meanwhile, back in the private sector, we have people and organizations with lots of money. Many of them see how they could have even more money if only the tax code were tweaked a bit in their favor, maybe regulations readjusted, perhaps a bill passed that helped their competitive position, a tariff placed on competing imports, and sometimes special programs to benefit a particular company or industry. Labor unions, which also have lots of money, want laws that tilt the labor-management negotiations more in their favor or that penalize foreign labor.

It is not difficult to see where this is going.

This does not suggest bribery is taking place, but it does suggest that money gets attention and creates a favorable bias. The people and organizations that make very large campaign contributions are not dumb; it's difficult to see why they would continue to contribute

---

104 "Pensions in Chili," Wikipedia. Original sources are listed there.
105 "Pensions in Australia," Wikipedia. Original sources are listed there.

over and over if they did not feel they were getting adequate return for their investment.

Congress is—and should be—castigated for supporting so many programs and situations that to other eyes seem indefensible. But Congressmen are in an almost untenable position; they are supposed to maintain an arm's length relation with the private sector and still raise money for their election campaigns. This duality of conflicting objectives does not make politicians blameless for postures that essentially ignore valid and recognizable national needs, but the structure of incentives they face is a reality that we have to understand if we are to successfully take action to improve the situation.

The result of this crony-capitalism is that we live with a very complex tax code and all its waste, with far too many regulations governing commerce, a few laws that we could do well without, and labor unions that are too powerful. The collaborative coziness that has developed between industry and government distorts competition by tilting the playing field.

It would be nice if the government could respond to private sector entreaties by just saying "No," but that hasn't worked here much better than it did in the back seat.[106]

Can We Alleviate the Problem with Finance Laws?

My personal instinct is that there is no help in restrictive finance laws; it is too difficult to come up with any acceptable system of restrictions that clever and motivated people can't game. I tend to favor no restrictions whatsoever on campaign contributions, the only requirement being prompt and total transparency as to where the money really comes from; this would allow the voters to judge the likely bias of a particular candidate based on whose money is providing support. For example, if the candidate accepts large sums

---

106 For readers under sixty: in the olden days the back seat of a car was often the only place available for teen-age sex.

from unions, it would be naïve to think that the candidate will not be a strong supporter of union causes, or the recipient of contributions from the oil industry would not be a supporter thereof. Transparency is impotent, however, unless the voters are paying attention.

Get the Money out of Politics

An alternative to private sector funding of campaigns is to have the taxpayer foot the bill, thus removing the need for any elected public servant to be beholden in any sense to private sector interests.[107] There would, of course, be a need for criteria for deciding who might be eligible for such funding, and a lot of other issues to be settled, but let us assume that a reasonable system could be devised.

Today there are two influences on a politician: first, the actual vote of the citizenry, and, second, the desires of the people and organizations who put up the money for his or her campaign.

What happens if we eliminate the moneyed interests? Now only the voters count. Now the political power advantage held by the less-rich voters is made even stronger, magnifying the problems of fiscal imprudence and rich-to-poor wealth transfer.

Currently that behavior is at least partially tempered by the private sector entities that contribute to campaigns, and which thereby gain some leverage over the path the country takes. While the pressure from these moneyed interests is selfish, they do not want to kill the economic goose that lays all the eggs because they are acutely aware that their own welfare is immediately tied to it. They will therefore oppose actions that threaten to do so. Neither do the voters who vote themselves goodies want to kill the goose, but too many think it indestructible and fail to recognize that their actions could be fatal to it.

---

107 Even this does not preclude influence through such things as, for example, promise of a high-paying job on leaving public service.

I fear that if nothing changes to better balance political power, removing all the influence of private sector money would encourage an even more debilitating level of overspending and progressive taxation. If political power could, by some magic, be made more balanced, then taxpayer financing of elections might be an effective step toward reducing crony capitalism.

I conclude that we are probably stalemated on actually getting the money out of politics anytime soon.

CHAPTER 6 - THE NEED FOR GROWTH

The United States, like most of the advanced nations today, is soon to become a victim of its changing demographics. The baby-boomers are leaving the work force and retiring. The result is an increase in the number of retirees without a compensating increase in the size of the work force that provides their support. So the number of aging mouths to feed is going up and the number of people available to feed them is not growing proportionately.

Using Bureau of Census data[108] one can get an idea of the size of the problem. Between 2010 and 2020 the number of people in the working age population (eighteen to sixty-five) for every person over sixty-five (retirees) is expected to drop by roughly 23 percent. If nothing else changes, workers would have to raise their federal tax contributions to Social Security and Medicare by 30 percent to maintain the same retiree benefits provided today.

In 2025 that figure rises to over 50 percent.

The states and local governments also have retirement programs. All will be affected in similar ways by these changing demographics.

The problem may be much worse than these numbers imply. The nation has done nothing about reducing the unfunded liabilities of the existing entitlement programs, and must pay increasing interest on the rising national debt. Forecasts of future obligations from

---

108 Bureau of the Census: Table NP2009-T2-C.xls

new programs now in place are eye-popping; the baby-boomer retirements only compound an already frightening situation. *To any person not believing political fiction, the total picture spelled out is the stuff of nightmares.*

These forecasts make it hard to see how the nation can avoid making economic growth a very high priority; we need a larger economic pie if we are not to have large segments of the population suffer a substantial decrease in their material welfare. Based on our actions to date, the nation seems to be oblivious to this grim future.

The Path to Faster Growth

The ability to switch the nation to a policy encouraging economic growth will require concurrence of the voting population. Indifference might allow many specific actions to be at least partially implemented, but *real success requires that the need for growth becomes a national state of mind.* At the moment the possibility seems remote.

At the risk of sounding like a broken record,[109] the most effective action in that direction would be a shift in Social Security funding from defined benefit toward defined contribution, as discussed in the last chapter. This would both motivate endorsement of the policy of growth as well contribute to its realization, because a defined contribution system creates funds for investment.

Gross domestic product (GDP) is the product of the average output per hour of labor—the labor productivity—multiplied by the total labor hours worked, the upper limit of which is roughly defined by the size of the labor force.

Possibilities for increasing the labor force include encouraging more elderly employment, allowing more immigration, and by bringing more of our minority population into the mainstream of our economic system. The diversion of more folks from nonproductive to productive

---

109 For readers under age thirty, a record is a flat plastic disk that was used to play music before CDs were invented. When one was broken it kept playing the same thing over and over.

tasks is an effective increase in the size of the labor force. Simplification of the tax code is a prime example; by reducing the burden of preparing tax returns it would free a lot of people to do other things.

Productivity improvement depends on innovation, both large and small. Healthy innovation depends on a high level of investment. Investment is attracted and risk is better tolerated by the prospect of large returns. Returns are enhanced by minimizing the restrictions and obstacles to their pursuit, and by eliminating taxes on their realization. Healthy investment requires confidence in the stability of policy, which cannot be established if potential investors sense the regulatory and tax codes are likely to change unpredictably in the future. Uncertainty introduces more risk and therefore inhibits investments.

Corporate taxes reduce the profit available to businesses for investment.

In general, the more extensive and detailed the regulation of the economy, the more commerce and innovation are inhibited.

Invigorating wealth creation will be helped by more prudent fiscal behavior by the government. The overwhelming political power of the less-rich promotes an incentive to spend too easily. Government spending drains funds from the private sector, and to the degree these are potential investment funds, growth is penalized. Overspending also creates debt, which requires the payment of interest.

A better-educated populace would produce both more potential entrepreneurs and a more competent and flexible labor force. Better education will not alter differences in opinions on resource allocation: for example, the different judgments as to how much of the GDP should be allocated to the safety net and to government supplied services such as healthcare, but education would give all points of view a better understanding of the implications of their choices, and thus make for more informed outcomes.

Few people disagree that education in this country needs to be drastically reformed. To get improvement aimed at increasing productivity now, the only option is a vigorous program motivating and supplying adult education. In the longer run, we have much more effective options. That is the subject of the next chapter.

The Coin Has Two Sides

There are many who are not really disturbed by the thought of a bit of shrinking in the slices in the pie. They ask: do we really want more wealth? They suggest that we have enough now; that maybe we should just slow down, and focus on improving our environment and making sure that everyone has a decent life. Some think maybe we should move toward the old Swedish model: accept much larger taxes, make them very progressive to increase equality, and then let a more paternalistic government take over many of the problems of living.[110]

We have, in fact, already moved a long way in that direction. The government has taken over substantial support for the aged through Social Security and Medicare. Now it has committed deeply to general healthcare for everybody. Over the years many other programs have been accumulating at all levels to provide support and medical care for children and for low income, unemployed, and disabled folks. All told, something like 40 percent of federal taxes collected are returned to the people under a variety of programs with the intent of improving lives.

Purposefully or not, we have been giving up growth. The rate of real GDP per capita increase from 1950 to 1970 was 2.29 percent. In the twenty years from 1970 to 1990 it was 2.19 percent. Now, in the last nineteen from 1990 to 2009 it dropped more markedly to 1.41 percent.[111] (The drop in the last nine years was obviously pulled down by the subprime recession in those years.)

---

110 This model got into financial trouble in the early 1990's, and has now been modified to reduce government spending and emphasize business competitiveness. *"Economy of Sweden,"* Wikipedia. References given are in Swedish.

111 From http://www.measuringworth.com/datasets/usgdp/result.php.

Doing Good is Expensive

Many people fail to appreciate how much "doing good" depends on a healthy economy. Wealth has allowed us to think and act differently. Attitudes toward charity have not softened because we are more generous than our great-grandparents, but because we can afford to be. We can afford social safety nets. We can be concerned about all the insults that man is said to be inflicting on the environment, because we can afford to be. A healthy economy is the foundation for it all.

Professor Jack Hollander makes a strong case that wealth, not poverty, is the real friend of the environment, that lifting the world out of poverty will do more for the environment than any other action. [112]

Wealth and affluence is not to be avoided to save the world; quite the opposite is true.

---

112 Jack M. Hollander is Emeritus Professor of Energy and Resources at the University of California at Berkeley. Hollander, *The Real Environmental Crisis: Why Poverty, Not Affluence, Is the Environment's Number One Enemy*, (2003)

Chapter 7 -
A Revolution In Education

The nation is in dire need of a much more effective education industry. A better education helps people be more comfortable in their own lives. A better education is important to democratic government, government whose effectiveness depends on the collective judgment of its people. A more versatile education industry is needed to produce a workforce that can support the growth we need and excel in the more competitive world we see ahead of us. A more adaptive education industry is mandatory if our inner city enclaves are ever to be integrated into the productive fabric of the nation.

Education is accomplished through many channels: on-the-job-training, experience, home schooling, the public K-12 system, private schools, colleges of all kinds, adult-education courses, and through many diverse resources such as the Khan Academy and The Teaching Company. Opportunities for education should be available throughout life.

Discussed here are the three that that in my judgment are the most blatantly deficient in our nation today: early on-the-job-training, the K-12 system, and education for the inner cities.

On-the-Job Training

For centuries the only education most people got was on-the-job-training. Apprentices would work, sometimes for years, to learn a trade. Usually they were paid nothing, and sometimes they even paid their employer for the privilege of learning.

On-the-job-training is still important today. Young people need to learn the fundamentals of getting and holding jobs: such simple things as the need to reliably show up for work on time; how to dress; how to interact with a boss, with fellow workers, and maybe with customers; how to handle a paycheck; and perhaps how to start learning a trade.

Such teenage training is particularly important for high school dropouts because by interfering with the opportunity to learn how to get and hold a legitimate job, the lesson being taught is how to survive on the streets without one. This is not a trivial problem: data from the state of California show some 33 percent of African Americans and 25 percent of Hispanic/Latinos dropping out of school during the last four years of K-12 education.[113]

The problem is that today minimum-wage laws make it illegal for anyone to work for pay below that specified by the law. Usually that figure is well above what the untrained individual is worth to a potential employer. The result is that too many teenagers never get hired.

In 2009, 39.5 percent of black teenagers couldn't find jobs, so failed to get that vital education. For Hispanics it was 30.2 percent, for Asians 26.4 percent, and for whites 21.8 percent.[114]

Attempts to fix prices at something other than the market-determined supply-demand price have almost always had unfortunate unintended consequences.[115] In this case fixing wages

---

113 This statement is based on the results for California cited in David A. Stuit and Jeffery A. Springer, "California's High School Dropouts, Examining the Fiscal Consequences," September 2010, sponsored by *The Foundation for Educational Choice*.

114 Bureau of Labor Statistics, Report 1026.

115 In the early 70s, anticipating a shortage that would drive up prices, the government fixed the price of gasoline. The result was long, wasteful lines of cars waiting for hours for gasoline in some places, while there was plenty in others. Fixing prices removed the signals that would have told where it was short and where it was plentiful, and removed the incentive to try to reallocate. It was painful. The next administration restored normal market-determined pricing and the problem went away.

above market leads to teen unemployment, and very possibly to many blighted lives.

The K-12 System

So far this book has been largely descriptive, occasionally analytical, and only mildly prescriptive. This section, though, just happens to be the hottest of the author's hot-button issues, and I cannot restrain myself from being very prescriptive. Be warned.

The public system of K-12 education, kindergarten through twelfth grade, is in deplorable shape. Our nation has far too many citizens who cannot read with real understanding, who cannot do simple math, who do not know how to think logically, and who do not understand even vaguely how the economy or the government works. The latter, absolutely necessary to be an intelligent voter, is not even part of many schools' curricula. We have a government shaped by "We the People," and do almost nothing to equip "us the people" to competently carry out the responsibility implied.

Statistics abound; a sample can be found in the results of the tests given every three years by the Program for International Student Assessment. These tests are given to fifteen-year-olds in sixty-five countries. In reading skill the US was seventeenth; Shanghai, China was first. In math the US was thirty-first; Shanghai, China was first. In science the US was twenty-third; Shanghai, China was first.[116]

There is little point in recounting more evidence of deficiencies; the situation has been amply publicized.

The primary problem is not at the top; the dedicated young people of our elite get reasonably good educations, although there are many stories about good schools still failing to challenge exceptional students. The primary concern here is the education being attained by the middle to lower end of our socioeconomic spectrum. It is obvious that here our government-supplied K-12 education system is flunking the course badly.

---

116 Published in the Wall Street Journal, Jan 8-9, 2011.

Governments and parents have spent decades trying to improve educational performance, with little impact. They've tried spending more money, tried more testing of students, and tried fighting with the teachers' unions over such issues as whether or not to pay good teachers more than bad.

The charter school movement is a slightly brighter spot. Charter schools are still public schools, operating on the same general model as other public schools, but with fewer restrictions. There is no question that allowing staff the freedom to manage intelligently generally produces better results.

With rules largely shaped by the teachers' unions, with dubious help from school boards, school personnel are hemmed in by rules and given responsibilities that are frustratingly inconsistent with their authority. *"The people running our public schools lack the basic tools of management that every business has: the discretion to reward their best staff with higher pay, to fire those who are incompetent, to allocate funds in ways that will have a maximum impact on student achievement."*[117]

The teachers' unions show more concern for the teachers than for the students. Its personnel policies are driven by seniority, not merit. Preservation and stability are more highly valued than adaptability and innovation. This from the President of the Fordham Foundation: *"The more time I spend in this field, the more appalled I become by the argument that no reform should even be tried unless and until its proponents can prove in advance that it will work perfectly and will have no adverse consequences or unwanted side effects."*[118]

Diagnoses abound: "we have to get the parents more involved", "we need more really good teachers," "we have to get rid of the unions," "classes are too big," "if we only had computers," "we need more money"

---

117 Thernstrom, Abigail and Stephan, *No Excuses: Closing the Racial Gap in Learning*, (2004), 166.

118 Chester E. Finn, Jr., President, Thomas B Fordham Foundation in the foreword of Richard K. Vedder, *Can Teachers Own Their Own Schools?*

The first one—that students need more parental support—is certainly a valid concern; parental attitude does matter a great deal. But parental attitudes are what they are, and are not going to be changed easily or quickly. The educational system has to work with the world as it is now, not as we wish it were. So schools have to learn how to successfully educate without back-up from parents. Excuses wear thin; decades have been spent trying to unravel the K-12 knot of failure. It is time to cut it.

A New K-12 Education Industry

If we were to start from scratch to design a system to deliver K-12 education, a sensible first step would be to examine the potential clientele: the kids and teenagers themselves. The first and obvious point is that they are all different. They have different mental equipment, different rates of maturation, are motivated differently, have different interests, learn differently, come from different environments and cultures, and get vastly different degrees of support from their parents or parent.

An obvious implication is that there is no one best way to teach. A variety of approaches tailored to these differences is needed if each individual is to reach their full potential. The definition of what constitutes a "school" needs to become much more flexible. Now the student is required to adapt to the school; we need an educational system that adapts the school to the student.

The current government-run system doesn't even come close to the flexible, adaptive system that is needed. In most areas the type of school a given student attends depends entirely on where he lives, not on his or her interest or capabilities. Most can only change schools by moving to another school district.

Is the current government-run K-12 system capable of being changed enough to provide the kind of education that is needed? Based on the difficulty to date in forcing much simpler improvements, the answer is a clear NO. The flexibility just isn't there: innovation is discouraged and any change that threatens teacher tenure or numbers is fought.

Organizations can seldom change themselves from the inside; it takes serious competitive threats from the outside to force the introspection and nerve needed for change. I believe that if the nation is to seriously improve its K-12 system, it has to establish a new student-tailored system of education by opening the field to the innovative dynamism of a competitive, minimally-regulated private sector. This could produce a K-12 education industry that is a day-over-night improvement over even the best of the current government-run establishments.

How?

The normal *modus operandi* of our free-market private sector is to find markets that are not being served adequately and serve them. In the context of schooling, the "markets" are children or teenagers who have a particular combination of goals and capabilities. The result will be a spectrum of "schools" that offer variety in both objectives and methods. Some would aim at teaching and stimulating high-IQ students; some would specialize in "problem" kids; still others would focus on supplying education to kids with special interests, kids who want to learn a trade, and so on. Probably most schools would operate by offering a menu of options within an establishment of wider focus.

If a private sector entrepreneur spots a class of kids whose particular needs and characteristics are not being best served, the business opportunity represented will drive him or her to serve that demand. That is normal behavior for the profit-driven, free-market private sector.

One can reasonably envision the private sector offering student-tailored education, delivered by techniques that take advantage of the best technology and ingenuity that a more innovative industry could bring to bear.

It is already happening. For example, there is a private sector company called Knewton that has developed software that lets on-line instruction automatically and in real time adapt to the learning style of the student; this effectively does adapt the lesson to the student. Knewton is not alone; there are many still-small companies that in one way or another are trying to make the transmission of knowledge more effective.[119]

The private sector is competitive, and competition drives innovation; one would expect to see the evolution of a wide variety of approaches to conveying knowledge. One would expect to see shameless copying of those that were particularly effective and rejection of those that were less so. Markets are heartless judges of what works and what doesn't. Private sector "schools" would always be a hot topic, kept in the public eye by the press, hundreds of blogs, and would be a common subject of conversation among parents. This is the consequence of variety and competition, and publicity will operate much faster to expose schools that are ineffective or misleading in their promises than the current system, where failing schools seem to be able to live forever.

A criticism of our government-run, union-dominated schools today is their slow and tentative exploitation of new technologies and techniques. If just a fraction of the creativity in the use of technology we see evidenced in the entertainment industry were directed toward better delivery of education, learning could be more efficient, more interesting, more fun, and more likely to be retained. Just think of how well teenagers remember the details of *Star Wars* or *Harry Potter and the Whatever* in comparison with the absorption and retention of last week's history lesson.

We say we need more truly gifted teachers. One way to get more is to multiply the reach and effectiveness of the ones we have. Technology allows this through a variety of media, and makes it possible to make

---

119 Bruce Upbin, *World's Greatest Tutor: Students learn differently, yet they're all taught the same way. Knewton has technology to adapt courses to kids.* Forbes, March 12, 2012. Also see http://www.knewton.com/about/

their talents broadly available. It's not quite the same as in the flesh, but advancing technology is making it closer and closer.

Technology allows more scope for the expression of creativity. Professor Hans Rosling of Sweden shows unusual creativity in how he tells a story with data.[120] He is an example of how creative thinking can be captured and made into a teaching tool. The teaching techniques and system developed by Salman Khan are exciting.[121] There are more: in development now are on-line books with embedded videos and even other books to turn them into a new kind of "dynamic information package."

I think one area that has significant promise to education is video gaming. The December 10, 2011 issue of The Economist has a ten page special report on gaming. There are dozens of variants: individual games at all levels of complexity, multi-person games, simulations, and virtual environments where the player "lives" in a fictional world. Their use has grown beyond just entertainment; they are now used as a management tool in business. The military uses them in training. But unless I missed it, in ten pages there was no mention of their use in K-12 education. With their obvious versatility games could be used in dozens of ways in teaching. The math learned through a competitive game is, I conjecture, more likely to be understood and remembered than that learned from a lecture. Game builders with their creativity could make many other subjects and educational situations both fun and understandable.[122] This is one more way of using technology to package creativity and ingenuity to enhance the productivity of teachers.

Throughout this book the story is being told of how the free-market and capitalism have brought us out of caves to the wealth we enjoy today. It has done so because it has motivated and enabled

---

120 Log on to http://www.ted.com/talks/view/id/92

121 See the Khan Academy. http://khanacademy.org/

122 From Google: "Star Journey. Take control of your spaceship and reach for the stars. Avoid obstacles and gravitational pulls of moons and black ... "; " over 3000 free online games! Including arcade games, puzzle games, funny games, sports games, shooting games, and more!"

people to do things differently, to innovate. The competitive market has been merciless in sorting the workable from the unworkable, the good approaches from the not so good. It makes little sense to not let the same free market forces that have worked so well in providing us with a wonderful variety of choices in our supermarkets weave their magic in creating a new K-12 education industry.

It can't be instantaneous; there will be a learning curve. There will be early successes, but also failures and undoubtedly some embarrassments. But problems will get solved; they won't persist for decade after decade, as they have with the nonresponsive public system. The end result could well be the best-educated citizenry that the world has ever seen.

What Will Let It Happen?

The short answer is a market big enough to attract the talent needed, to induce the major companies already in the educational business to set up K-12 divisions, and entice new entries like Microsoft or Google or Disney or Macmillan—and probably dozens of companies that I haven't thought of. There would also be lots of small start-ups by entrepreneurs who spot opportunity.

K-12 education should continue to be financed by the taxpayer, just as it is now. No preference should be given to either government-run or private sector schools; both should each receive the same funding per student. The intent is to let the parents—no doubt in collaboration with their children—chose without bias the school they think best. To that end, parents should be given a voucher for each school-age child that lets them enter the school of their choice, either public or private. Thus the public schools are put in direct competition with the private sector schools.

Private sector schools would probably takeoff slowly—people are reluctant to change from the familiar—the devil you know—so most parents would be wary at first. Further, the public schools would react to the budding competition by seriously trying to clean up their act and become more competitive.

How big could this market be? The total cost of K-12 education in public school in 2009 was $562 billion. This was to educate just under 50 million students at an average cost per student of roughly $12 thousand.[123]

Assume, quite arbitrarily, that the competition more or less equalizes at a fifty-fifty distribution between public and private institutions. This would result in a private sector market of $240-$300 billion, roughly equivalent in size to fifteen or so Microsoft Corporations. That should be large enough to attract talent and entrepreneurs.

The opening of the K-12 educational industry to the private sector would also motivate an educational tool industry. There are many new and amazing technologies that could be exploited to produce a very large palette of new teaching tools—lecture videos, simulations, dynamic "books", both individual and competitive teaching games, and things I haven't thought of. A new market in educational tools would motivate a redirection of some of the minds that created all those clever computer games and Wii systems and simulations toward the goal of aiding K-12 education. The judicious use of these tools should make it possible to deliver excellent education much faster, more efficiently, and more painlessly than has ever been possible.

It won't happen unless the private sector had a high level of confidence that such a national voucher system would be stable over a number of years, not subject to easy cancellation. Without that confidence businesses will be very reluctant to risk the high start-up costs necessary to enter the field. How this can be accomplished is beyond the author's pay-grade; I do not know how any administration can provide reasonable assurance that a program will not be significantly modified by a future administration. The

---

123 Center for Education Reform—K-12 Facts; http://www.edreform.com/Fast_Facts/ K12_Facts/.

fact that so many government programs seem impossible to turn off gives some hope that it can be done.

Current voucher programs do not in any way illustrate the potential that is envisioned here: they are too small to attract the interest of new entrepreneurs or set the stage for real competition, and they have too many strings attached that prevent real innovation. They may actually be a detriment to instituting a large-scale national program, in that people may assume that the small improvement in performance they demonstrate is typical of what can be expected from a competitive, relatively unrestricted, nation-wide voucher-financed K-12 education industry.

Quality Control

In order to insure that all students complete their K-12 program equipped with a well-rounded education, it will be necessary to define a minimum curriculum that all 'schools' must include. This will not be easy. Richard Riley, when he was the U. S. Secretary of Education in 2004, wrote, "*We are currently preparing students for jobs that don't yet exist, using technologies that haven't been invented, in order to so solve problems we don't even know are problems yet.*"

There are two implications of that truth that immediately come to mind. First, the most crucial requirement to be able to adapt to a rapidly changing and partially unpredictable future is learning how to think logically. Second, every citizen will more comfortable in this increasingly technical world if they have some basic knowledge of the sciences.

We haven't yet learned to cope with democracy—how to competently run a nation in which the citizens are in charge. It is very clear that today only a distinct minority of citizens really understand how the government and the economy function, and have more than the most superficial knowledge of history and current affairs in the international arena. In an ideal future everyone needs the knowledge to both make the most of their own lives and endeavors, but to also to be a responsible citizen.

The only way to assure that students are learning is through testing. Frequent testing will be necessary to measure progress toward mastery of this minimum curriculum, and final tests would be one of the criteria for graduation. These tests should administered in a way that is totally independent of the various schools themselves.

One approach to carrying out this test design and administration functions might be through the establishment of a dedicated national testing service. There is as much opportunity for innovation in test design as in the development of teaching tools and techniques.; this could be tapped by having tests at least partially procured through competitive bidding.

This organization might also define and lead the very broad process for defining and maintaining the minimum curriculum.

This organization would not, however, be responsible in any way for the techniques the various schools choose to use for actual teaching, nor allowed to interfere with that process other than to administer tests.

Another, and very important, element of quality control is public opinion. There will be a strong spotlight on the workings of this new industry. Mentioned earlier and amplified here, that spotlight will be turned on by the high level of interest such a new program of national importance is likely to engender. The sheer diversity of this new approach will make it a much more common topic of general conversation. It will attract attention through the press, blogs, Facebook, Twitter, academic studies, and the advertising done by the schools themselves as they compete for students.

A common question is how, without close supervision by the government, would kooks with outlandish ideas be prevented from setting up "schools" and teaching their weird notions? Or illegal things, like terrorism.

Both the market spotlight and the independent progress testing should help warn of problems. It also might be sensible to require some screening by standardized psychological testing of the principle personnel involved in any of these schools (or perhaps not).

Governments at all levels are going to want to impose requirements for and restrictions on how these private sector schools operate, to impose their wisdom "to protect the children." This should be resisted strongly. There will be some lost sheep, with or without government regulation, but with regulation much of the potential advantage of private sector ingenuity and innovation and potential for truly radical improvement in K-12 education will be compromised, perhaps fatally. Government interference is dangerous; once the government inserts itself, it is in the nature of government to want to expand its role. [124]

Inner City Education

A portion of our populace, mostly minorities, is trapped in sub-cultures that contribute little to national well-being, and in fact drains from it. The nation needs to break this cycle; it needs to bring everybody into productive society.

The way to do it is to start at the bottom: change the kids and the next generation will be on a new path. The only way I can think of to do that is through a different kind of education.

The primary education problem appears to be lack of dedicated parental support and positive guidance. The *Knowledge is Power Program* (KIPP) schools show what can be done if there is parental support. There are now ninety-nine of these schools scattered around the country serving twenty-seven thousand students. Aimed almost exclusively at lower-income families of color, they claim a

---

124 See *Camel's noses*, Wikipedia.

track record of having 85 percent of students who completed their eighth grade at KIPP continuing on to college.[125]

But without parental support the cards are stacked against today's schools: they are competing for attention with the street culture. Teachers have to devote more effort to controlling behavior than to educating. The (Philadelphia) Inquirer's series "Assault on Learning" (March 2011) reported that in the 2010 school year, "690 teachers were assaulted; in the last five years, 4,000 were." The newspaper reported that in Philadelphia's 268 schools, "on an average day 25 students, teachers, or other staff members were beaten, robbed, sexually assaulted, or victims of other violent crimes. That doesn't even include thousands more who are extorted, threatened, or bullied in a school year." [126]

There are a few success-story schools, but it's a tough environment for education and such stories are rare. It is probably true that that most inner city schools are under-funded, but few believe just providing more money would make much difference.

One way, possibly the only way, to provide the kids in these enclaves with real educational opportunity is to take them completely out of their normal environment at various intervals and expose them to a completely different one, an experience that might open their eyes to a new view of the world and of their lives. Put them in a completely new environment, expose them to a larger reality, surround them with potential role models that are teaching and working with them, showing them how to behave and how to think logically, and setting high expectations. The objective is to provide not only a conventional education but a whole perspective and behavior-altering experience.

This experience has to be so attractive that the kids really want to participate, so the very prospect is motivation for improved performance. The time period would vary with age, ranging for

---

125 "Q and A: KIPP Adeline and the Charter School Experience," *The San Diego Union Tribune*, April 10, 2011. See www.kipp.org.
126 From Walter Williams, *Rising Black Social Pathology*.

each episode from perhaps a week for the very young to maybe two to three months for the older teenagers. Obviously the parents have to accept and approve of the idea.[127]

Here a few approaches are put forward just to illustrate the thinking; a competitive private sector should have better ideas.

An obvious approach is putting the kids in dude-ranch type facilities in which the kids, of course under supervision, would have the responsibility of operating—caring for the animals, doing the cooking and serving, cleaning up, housekeeping—and getting educated. It is an opportunity to teach life: the behavior and deportment that will be needed to function well in the wider world. There would be continuous interaction with role models. The opportunity is there to take advantage of all kinds of new teaching tools and techniques and to better mix learning with daily activities.

A few back-of-the-envelope numbers show that only a fraction of inner city kids could be accommodated in this kind of program; it doesn't lend itself to handling thousands at a time. So participation has to be treated as something special: a prize that only a fraction can win.

Another possibility is to provide a series of living-teaching facilities in different cities that groups could rotate through, spending a few weeks, more or less, in each, becoming in essence student-tourists. Part of the curriculum would be visits to various industries, exposure to various trades, perhaps some community colleges, or universities, and spots of historical significance.

A more far-out idea appeals to my imagination: at one or more points in their schooling put a selected group of kids on old cruise ships that have been modified to serve as floating venues for these behavior- and perspective-altering educations. I know a very bright and dedicated lady who has been teaching in an inner-city school for some years. Here, briefly, is what she thought of this idea.

---

127 Parental approval should be completely voluntary, and the separation temporary, the period depending on age. Years ago both the U.S. and Australia have tried separation programs with the same objective, but in these the children were taken forcibly and permanently. The programs were disasters.

"You open all kinds of possibilities. Marine biology, math, mapping, geography, history—they would all mean something... I love the idea."

Then the cold water: "The cost to do this would be ridiculous." She is certainly right; it would be very expensive. But if a successful formula could be found that would begin to bring our inner city cultures into the main stream of national life, it almost wouldn't matter what it cost, because the cost of not doing it is today now so overwhelming in so many dimensions: crime, drugs, human misery, lost productivity, and a culture unbefitting a great, unified nation.

Mix and match schemes would evolve using for all these possibilities, including tuned-up conventional schools, using various combinations for kids at different ages.

Whatever the venue, surround the kids with role models to help remold their behavior and values, mixing teaching with living, and let them see that a bigger and better world is open to them.

CHAPTER 8 - CAN
CAPITALISM SURVIVE?

"Can capitalism survive?
No. I do not think it can".
Joseph Schumpeter[128]

Of course it can; there is very little chance that this country will imitate Cuba or the old USSR. But can it survive in good health, and continue to produce wealth as abundantly as it has in the past? That is the question that Professor Schumpeter was addressing, and the answer is very much open to doubt.

In the late eighteenth century a few nations started demonstrating that scarcity did not have to be the dominant theme of existence, that reasonably permissive and competent governments, free people with guaranteed property rights, free and open markets, and capitalist finance could turn creativity and enterprise into wealth. What had been a whisper became a shout.

Free market capitalism is a huge success: by any comparison with the rest of the world, the capitalist nations are rich. The poverty levels in advanced capitalist nations are probably well above the median income of the rest of the world.

---

128 Thomas K. McCraw, Emeritus Professor of Business History in the Harvard Business School, interprets this answer as more a stratagem to induce to an open mind in the reader than to render a positive judgment. McCraw, Prophet of Innovation: Joseph Schumpeter and Creative Destruction, (2007), 351.

In the last forty years or so, the lure of capitalist abundance has induced country after country to introduce capitalistic practices. Mao Zedong died in 1976, and twelve years later Ding Xiaoping led an economically failed China to dip its toe into capitalism. The USSR broke up in 1991, freeing the Soviet block to turn capitalist. That same year India began its transition toward a more capitalist economic policy. These transforming nations hold at least three billion people,[129] almost half the population of the earth.

The world still has a long way to go. The transition will be slow and very probably turbulent. But capitalist abundance is a powerful lure, and will provide a continuing incentive to evolve in that direction; the odds look good that this will be the century in which most of the world adopts free market and capitalist practices. This new capitalist world is becoming a collection of experiments in how the level and kind of state participation in market-driven capitalism affects economic performance.

In his insightful and optimistic book, *The Age of Declining Turbulence*, Douglas N. Thompson labels this new phase for the world "The Awakening." It seems appropriate.

The Competitive Capitalist Century

Given unfettered trade among nations, the larger markets, growing affluence, and increasing numbers of innovating participants should offer greater opportunities for specialization, innovation, and economies of scale. The result should be an increase in standards of living everywhere in the capitalist world, higher than any single nation could have achieved alone with its more restricted market.

It won't happen without free trade. That is a tall order; just as happens today, our nation can reasonably expect continuing pressures for trade restrictions from both labor unions and

---

129 Bradley, Foster & Sargent, Inc., Quarterly Market Commentary, Oct. 2007. http://www. bfsinvest.com/pdf/3_2007a.pdf.

industries feeling the heat of foreign competition. But change does happen, and some success in opening markets is already apparent. According to the Business Roundtable, in 2001 there were about 130 Free Trade Areas[130] in the world. By 2009 the number had grown to over 300, with more in negotiation. Over 50 percent of world trade was through these Free Trade Areas.[131]

As spreading capitalism accelerates growth all over the world, the market for products at the high end of technological capability will expand far beyond current levels. This represents a huge potential market of many dimensions. Our multinational corporations are already exploiting this growing opportunity, but with more nations in the game, the competition will be coming from more directions.

Our current situation is not encouraging. Our government impedes commerce with excessive and inappropriate regulation, and penalizes capital formation both by bad tax policy and by diverting potential investment into other uses. Fear of union power has led to an inability to do anything about a K-12 education system that has persistently failed to produce a truly competitive work force and a well-informed electorate. Unbalanced political power results in a bias toward too much spending, too much debt, and an inability to face and act to restructure commitments with runaway costs.

As already discussed at length, the politicians we blame are behaving as the majority of people want them to behave, and they are almost forced by the election process to too-easily oblige the private sector in order to raise campaign money.

To put this situation in perspective, we need to remind ourselves that our nation is one of the older experiments in combining capitalism and democracy. We are now a little over two centuries into that experiment. We know what has happened thus far. The

---

130 A free trade area (FTA) is a trade bloc whose member countries have signed a free trade agreement (FTA), which eliminates tariffs, import quotas, and preferences on most (if not all) goods and services traded between them.

131 Thompson, The Age of Declining Turbulence, (2009), 31.

question now is how in the future do we best alleviate the problems that have manifested themselves?

It is not in the cards to return to the narrow definition of voter eligibility that was in place when the Constitution was adopted, nor does it look politically feasible to make any serious modifications to the voter franchise as it exists today. There are, however, actions within reach that could make a dramatic difference in our nation's future, already identified in earlier chapters.

The first is to give everyone an obvious and substantial stake in the performance of the economy. As described in Chapter 5, this can be done by transitioning the now defined-benefit Social Security system into a defined-contribution system. With this change, everyone's retirement contributions would be invested in the economy; if the economy thrived and grew, then the retirements would be far superior to what is now provided by the current system. If it did not, then the retirement benefits would be smaller. This provides an obvious motivation for everyone to care how the economy behaved, to watch it, and to be sensitive to actions and policies that affect it.

The second action is to remove all minimum wage laws that are preventing our teenagers from learning how to get and hold jobs. As pointed out in Chapter 7, the number of young people whose futures are being penalized by these laws is disgraceful.

The third action is to improve our K-12 education; this was discussed in Chapter 7. Today many of our citizens have already been cheated of a good education by poorly performing schools. We currently have to import a significant part of our technological talent. The nation still has subcultures that need to be brought into the broader fabric of society. We have ballots printed in many languages, implying we also have citizens who vote without understanding the English in which the nation's affairs are conducted and reported.

I believe a renaissance of education in our country is absolutely vital to our future. By letting the private sector introduce both competition and new sources of flexibility, ingenuity, and creativity into the K-12 education we can turn a government monopoly into a new, dynamic industry. It is my belief that we could provide our future citizens and leaders with education and skills superior to any the world has ever seen. The result would be a citizenry well equipped to carry out their civic responsibilities and to lead more satisfying and constructive lives.

There has never been a large nation in which all of the citizens were both truly well educated in how the government and the economy functioned and were also motivated to vigilantly monitor government behavior. With all the other advantages our nation possesses, the United States of America could become a model for a better world. We have a populace accustomed to freedom, to initiative, to competition, and to creative entrepreneurship and innovation. We already command a leadership position in the world. With markets expanding globally, a superbly educated populace, a more moderate regulatory regime, a simpler and more investment-friendly tax code, and a more fiscally prudent government, the prospects for our future could be very bright.

Can capitalism survive? Certainly it can. It can not only survive, it can improve.

Appendix A - Technology And Innovation

Many people look around at all the marvelous things that have already been invented, try to think of something fundamentally new, and, failing that, conclude that it's all been done, that there is nothing left to invent.

That is not a new delusion. Professor Schumpeter wrote more than seventy years ago of *"the widely accepted view that the great stride in technological advance has been made and that but minor achievements remain."*[132] That was before the discovery of the nuclear fission, the transistor, the laser, or DNA, all four of which have formed the trunks of innovation trees that have yielded multiple, still-growing branches.

We do not know what still lies *"in the lap of the gods."*[133] But with scientists pushing out the boundaries of knowledge in almost every field, it's hard to believe there is nothing more out there except new combinations and improvements of old stuff.

A different concern from running out of new things, though, is running out of new things that create jobs, particularly jobs for low and only moderately skilled labor. This concern is natural when the current trend is clearly to replace labor with technology. For example, machines that automatically do repetitive things have been with us for a long time. More and more, though, these machines—

---

132 Schumpeter, Capitalism, Socialism and Democracy, (1942), 117.
133 Ibid 118.

ᵊ becoming flexible, and are able to do a variety of tasks. ₊. ᴜne very real prospect of much cheaper energy in the future, the operating cost of flexibly automated machinery will come down, increasing its competitiveness with human workers.

We haven't stopped discovering things. There will almost surely be new kinds of jobs, activities of which we are not now aware. I have no convictions about the future: lots of trends unfolding on uncertain timetables with uncertain implications. Humans will be better educated; robots will be more capable. I think our real concern will be our ability to maintain a culture, a motivation, and an economy that is hospitable to discovery and innovation.

Almost for entertainment, I offer some possibilities for future developments that I consider interesting.

Some Conjectures—Driverless Vehicles

Within a decade we should have vehicles on our roads and highways without drivers. These self-chauffeuring vehicles will be safer than human drivers. They can react much faster than humans, and depend on sensors that don't fall asleep or get distracted by the kids in the back seat. People will still be able to drive them manually if they choose, but the system will prevent dangerous maneuvers. In the future anyone can "drive": eight or eighty, drunk or sober.

These new vehicles will have a huge impact on the economics of goods movement, on changing the demands for parking spaces, and on flexibility in location of homes and activities.[134] For example, the necessity to have parking within walking distance of one's destination forces acres of parking lots around malls, city streets full of cars looking for places to park or using high-priced real estate to provide that parking, and devoting an extra room in every home to the automobile(s). With the automated car, it can just drop the passengers, then go off for perhaps miles to park itself and wait until it's called back for pickup.

---

134 Garrison and Ward, *Tomorrow's Transportation*, 9-25

Some Conjectures—New Cities

Last century was the suburban century. The automobile and truck let people escape crowded cities and create suburbs. Businesses then followed the people, and the modern city with very extensive suburbs replaced the compact city designed around walking and mass-movement transportation. We now may be on the verge of another rearrangement in the way we live and work.

The next evolutionary step will very possibly be the redesign of our city cores. Currently there is often acute congestion caused by too many vehicles and the interference caused by mixing vehicle and pedestrian traffic. This interference can be eliminated by moving pedestrian traffic to different levels within urban structures. These would be connected by enclosed "bridges" over the streets. Moving walkways, escalators, and elevators, plus new forms of internal transportation on the pedestrian levels could provide easy movement over the whole integrated downtown complex.

Just as businesses followed people into the suburbs, businesses and shops would follow pedestrians—the shoppers—to the second floor. The city core would segregate into a vehicle level and a pedestrian level.

Parking would be on the periphery—or anywhere, since driverless cars could be sent away to park and called back for pickup.

There are people who like urban living, some who prefer suburban living, and some who would be happier with isolated living. There is no reason that we can't have all three, but until very recently the last was difficult for most people because their work, education, and social lives dictated their presence in the city. Further improvements in communication imply that proximity is less and less needed for satisfactory social and business interchange. That freedom of location would be further enhanced by the mobility implied by the driverless cars and a much broader gamut of mobile services. After some ten or so centuries in which the urban proportion of the population was growing, the technologies that have the potential to reverse this trend are within reach.

Some Conjectures—Desert conversion

The western part of the nation has huge areas that are empty. They are empty because they have no water. Given water, they would bloom. An interesting thought was suggested by my friend, Don Dawson, of Palos Verdes Estates, California: develop desalinating pipes, so that when salt water from the Pacific has been pumped a few hundred miles it comes out fresh. As the price of fresh water comes down the possibility for deserts to be made attractively livable opens up.

More

What fewer of us see are the dramatic innovations now on-going in the biological and medical arenas. The discovery of DNA only about sixty years ago opened doors to a whole new understanding of the body, and a different perspective on pharmaceutical drug design.

Science continues to advance across the board, and new discoveries inspire creativity. We are a very long way from running out of prospects for continuing innovation.

ACKNOWLEDGMENTS

First to Joseph A. Schumpeter, for igniting my interest in the subject with his *Capitalism, Socialism, and Democracy* many, many years ago.

Much more recently, my thanks to William L. Garrison, Professor Emeritus at the University of California at Berkeley. My e-mail conversations with Bill provided me with insights and perspectives that were extremely helpful in shaping this book, as were his commentaries on various versions of the manuscript. Many would describe Bill as one of the rare people who could truly think outside the box. I think that is an understatement; Bill doesn't know that there is a box.

I would also like to acknowledge the help of Charlotte Holmes with her comments on a very early manuscript. They were encouraging to me. Troy Miller helped me with repeated reviews of the material at various stages. I know he invested many hours in my project, and prevented me from making some embarrassing errors. Don Dawson helped with some very careful editing.

The editor at CreateSpace was very good and offered many valid and substantive comments that have been very helpful to me. She is not responsible for my substituting the Ward Manual of Style for the Chicago version thereof.

Last, my wife Penny had many very insightful suggestions that I've gratefully incorporated. She is a perceptive lady, and her advice has been very constructive.

About The Author

I have a BS in Physics from Caltech and, in my 40's, took a year off from real life to earn a Masters in Business Economics from UCLA. My forte throughout my several careers has been operations analysis and the synthesis of systems. My studies at UCLA ignited a real interest in economics, which I discovered is really operations analysis for grown-ups.

For years—usually late at night with a little wine—I sometimes puzzled with friends over the question of why, for thousands and thousands of years, very little seemed to change in terms of the material lives of average people, then all of a sudden we had an Industrial Revolution. It only began to make sense to me when I thought about change in the context of its historical evolution. One thought lead to another, and out came this book.

I am also coauthor with Bill Garrison of *Tomorrow's Transportation: Changing Cities, Economies, and Lives*, published in 2000 by Artech House.

I am now retired and living in San Diego with my wife Penny and our two poodles, Britain and Paris.

BIBLIOGRAPHY & REFERENCES

Allen, Robert C., *Progress and Poverty in Early Modern Europe.* Workshop Paper, Neufield College, Oxford, England, 2003. http://tuvalu.santafe.edu/events/workshops/images/8/81/ProgressPoverty.pdf.

Barnes, Craig S., *Democracy at the Crossroads.* (Golden, CO, Fulcrum Publishing, 2009).

Bartlett, Kenneth R., *The Development of European Civilization.* (The Great Courses, The Teaching Company, 2011).

Bosworth, Michael L., (1999). *The Rise and Fall of Chinese Seapower.* http://www.basicrps.com/chine/histoire/china.htm.

Carboni, G., *The History of Writing.* (Translation edited by Karyn Loscocco, September 2008, Revised in August 2011). http://www.funsci.com/fun3_en/writing/writing.htm

Cassidy, John, "What Good is Wall Street" *The New Yorker*, Nov 29, 2010.

Casson, Lionel O., *The Ancient Mariners: Seafarers and Sea Fighters in the Mediterranean in Ancient Times.* Second Edition (Princeton, NJ, Princeton University Press, 1991)

Christian, David, *Big History: The Big Bang, Life on Earth, and the Rise of Humanity.* (The Great Courses, The Teaching Company, Chantilly, VA., 2008).

Diamond, Jared, *Guns, Germs, and Steel: The Fates of Human Societies.* (W.W. Norton and Company, 1999)

Durant, Will, *The Life of Greece.* (New York, Simon and Schuster, 1939).

Durant, Will, *Caesar and Christ.* (New York, Simon and Schuster, 1944).

Durant, Will. *The Age of Faith.* (New York, Simon & Schuster, 1950).

Durant, Will and Ariel, *The Lessons of History.* (New York, Simon & Schuster, 1968).

Evans, L.T., *Feeding the Ten Billion.* (Cambridge University Press, 1998).

Encyclopedia Britannica, *Sumer.* http://www.britannica.com/EBchecked/topic/573176/Sumer

Fagan, Brian M., *World Prehistory: A Brief Introduction.* 7th edition, (Pearson Prentice Hall, 2008).

Firestone, Harvey S., Jr., *Man on the Move: The Story of Transportation,* (New York, G. P. Putman's Sons, 1967).

Ferguson, Niall, *The Ascent of Money: A Financial History of the World.* (Penguin Books, 2008)

Garrett, Thomas A. and Rhine, Russell M., "Social Security versus Private Retirement Accounts: A Historical Analysis." Federal Reserve Bank of St. Louis *Review*, March/April 2005, 87(2, Part 1).

Garrison, William L. and Ward, Jerry D., *Tomorrow's Transportation: Changing Cities, Economies, and Lives.* (Boston, Artech House, 2000).

Hayes, David, *Are Federal Regulations Too Numerous? Has The Number of Them Multiplied Excessively?* Writings of David Hayes, http://extent-of-regulation.dhwritings.com/.

Hayek, Friedrich, "The Use of Knowledge in Society," *American Economic Review, XXXV,* No. 4; September, 1945.

Henderson, David, *"Are Taxes on Corporations Paid by People."* Library of Economics and History, www.econlog.org.

Jack M. Hollander, *The Real Environmental Crisis: Why Poverty, Not Affluence, Is the Environment's Number One Enemy.* (Berkeley, The University of California Press, 2003).

Ikenson, Daniel J. & Lincicome, Scott, *"Beyond Exports: A Better Case for Free Trade"*, Cato Institute, Free Trade Bulletin no. 43.

Knight, Frank H., "Historical and Theoretical Issues in the Problem of Modern Capitalism," *Journal of Economics and Business History*, Nov. 1928

Knight, Frank H., *On the History and Method of Economics* (Chicago: University of Chicago Press, 1956).

Landes, David S.; Mokyr, Joel; Baumol, William J., *The Invention of Enterprise: Entrepreneurship from Ancient Mesopotamia to Modern Times.* (Princeton University Press, 2010).

Lipman, Francine J. James E. Williamson, Orange County Lawyer, May 2011. Available at SSRN: http://ssrn.com/abstract=1826404

Maudlin, John, "The Plight of the Working Class," April 2, 2011, The Big Picture Blog.

Mayor, Thomas, Hunter Gathers: The Original Libertarians. (*The Independent Review*, vol. 16, Num. 4, Spring 2012)

McCraw, Thomas K., *Prophet of Innovation: Joseph Schumpeter and Creative Destruction.* (The Bellnap Press of Harvard University Press, 2007)

McKinnon, John D., "High-Earning Households Pay Growing Share of Taxes." *Wall Street Journal*, May 3, 2011.

Mokyr, Joel, *The Lever of Riches.* (Oxford University Press, 1990).

Mokyr, Joel, *The Enlightened Economy: An Economic History of Britain 1700-1850.* (New Haven and London, Yale University Press, 2009).

Mummert, Amanda et al, Robusticity during the agricultural transition: Evidence from the bioarchaeological record. *Journal of Economics and Human Biology.* (Elsevier, 2011) http://www.scribd.com/doc/57927121/Stature-and-robusticity-during-the-agricultural-transition

Nasar, Sylvia, *Grand Pursuit: The Story of Economic Genius.* (Simon and Schuster, 2011)

Noble, Thomas F. X., *The Foundations of Western Civilization*, (The Great Courses, The Teaching Company, 2002).

North, Douglass C. & Thomas, Robert Paul, *The Rise of the Western World: A New Economic History.* (Cambridge University Press, 1973).

North, Douglass C., *Structure and Change in Economic History.* (New York: W.W. Norton and Co., 1981).

Perry, Mark J., "U.S. Manufacturing: More Output from Fewer Workers," *Seeking Alpha*, April 26, 2009.

Perry, Mark J., *Income Inequality can be explained by Household Demographics*, The Enterprise Blog, using CBO data. Oct 21, 2011),

Saalman. Howard, *Medieval Cities.* (New York: George Brazillar, 1968).

Schumpeter, Joseph, *Capitalism, Socialism and Democracy.* (Harper Colophon Books, 1950).

Stuit, David A. and Springer, Jeffery A., *"California's High School Dropouts, Examining the Fiscal Consequences."* Sponsored by The Foundation for Educational Choice, September 2010.

Joel Tarr, Urban Pollution: Many Long Years Ago. *American Heritage* XXII, (Oct. 1971)

Taylor, Timothy, *Herbert Hoover, Deficit-Spender: Correcting John Judis in The New Republic*, Conversable Economist Blog, Sept 28, 2011. http://conversableeconomist.blogspot.com/2011/09/herbert-hoover-deficit-spender.html

Thernstrom, Abigail and Stephan, *No Excuses: Closing the Racial Gap in Learning.* (Simon and Schuster, 2004).

Thompson, Douglas N., *The Age of Declining Turbulence*, (Salt Lake City, Crossroads Research Institute, 2009).

Tuchman, Barbara W. *A Distant Mirror: The Calamitous Fourteenth Century.* (Ballantine, 1978).

Vaughn's Summaries, Vaughn Aubuchon, World Population Growth Histories. www.vaughns-1-pagers.com/history/world-population-growth.htm.

Vedder, Richard K., Taxes Fuel Historic American Migration. *The Heartland Institute.* http://news.heartland.org/newspaper-article/2005/12/01/taxes-fuel-historic-american-migration.

Vedder, Richard K., *"Can Teachers Own Their Own Schools?* New Strategies for Educational Excellence," (Oakland, CA., The Independent Institute, 2000).

Voigt, Kevin, *Monkey Business: Jungle Economics*, CNN, November 4, 2009. http://edition.cnn.com/2009/WORLD/asiapcf/11/02/economics.monkey.business/index.html

Wattenberg, Caplow, and Hicks, *The First Measured Century.* (Washington, DC. American Enterprise Institute for Public Policy Research, 2001).

Whitten, David O., The Recession of 1893. Auburn University. posted on the internet by the *Economic History Association.*

White Jr., Lynn, *Medieval Technology and Social Change,* (London, Oxford University Press, 1962)

Williams, Walter, *Rising Black Social Pathology.* Townhall (2/15/2012) http://townhall.com/columnists/walterewilliams/2012/02/15/rising_black_social_pathology

INDEX

CPSIA information can be obtained at www.ICGtesting.com
Printed in the USA
LVOW11s1529040414

380379LV00011B/578/P